More Praise for *Ask, Listen, Act*

"Twenty years ago, Luz blew into my life with her deep compassion, amazing creativity, and heart the size of a washtub. She stood philanthropy on its head, asking grantees what they needed rather than telling them what they needed. This book about her incredible life is a must-read."

—Representative Pat Schroeder,
Colorado's 1st District (1973–1997)

"Over the course of her forty-year career, Luz Vega-Marquis has charted her own path in philanthropy by taking her lead from low-income communities of color. Now, as those communities face unprecedented challenges, she offers an urgent mandate for philanthropy to return to its roots in the love of humanity, support for grassroots organizing, and the necessity of developing new leaders, especially women of color. Anyone whose life or work has been touched by philanthropy—and everyone who has confronted poverty, racism, or inequality—should read this book."

—Dorian Warren, president of Community Change

"Luz Vega-Marquis is a bold leader who joined philanthropy with a vision to reinvent it. Her journey from a Nicaraguan village to becoming the first Latinx leader for a large philanthropy shows why reflective leadership matters. This book is a must-read for anyone who cares about racial and economic equity."

—Nichole June Maher, president and CEO,
Group Health Foundation

T0125487

"Luz Vega-Marquis taps into her immigrant background and the struggles of her family, channels her experiences in social justice, and asserts deep and meaningful listening and engaging of community leaders—to lift a new way forward for organized philanthropy. Her message: if philanthropy is to be successful in addressing structural inequality, remember that heart, courage, storytelling, and humility will carry far more impact value than intellectual rigor and clever analysis."

—Robert K. Ross MD, president and CEO
of the California Endowment

"Ever since I met Luz about fifteen years ago I became enthralled by her personal story of womanhood, activism, and leadership. I asked her to talk about herself more often but Luz said no, the attention needed to be on working families. I am thrilled that now Luz has finally shared her story of power-hood with the world. On many occasions I would ask myself 'what would Luz do?' This book provides many answers and lessons. Luz taught me, and this book reinforces, the concept of power and humility existing in leadership at the same time."

—Maria Hinojosa, anchor and executive producer,
Latino USA on National Public Radio

"In this timely new book, Luz Vega-Marquis shares her powerful personal story and shines a light on America's working families and their struggle for survival and empowerment in a time of rampant inequality. By highlighting the growing family movement to achieve voice, power, and policy change, Vega-Marquis challenges policymakers and philanthropic leaders to address systemic inequality, now."

—Jesús G. "Chuy" García, U.S. Representative
for Illinois's 4th District

Luz Vega-Marquis is the founding president and chief executive officer of the Marguerite Casey Foundation. She is the founder of Hispanics in Philanthropy and has served on numerous boards of directors. She lives in Seattle, Washington. This is her first book.

ASK, LISTEN, ACT

ASK, LISTEN, ACT

A NEW MODEL FOR PHILANTHROPY

LUZ VEGA-MARQUIS

JACQUES BOOKS

© 2020 by Marguerite Casey Foundation
All rights reserved.
No part of this book may be reproduced, in any form, without written permission from the
publisher.

Published in the United States by Jacques Books, an imprint of The New Press,
New York, 2020
Distributed by Two Rivers Distribution

ISBN 978-1-62097-634-0 (pb)
ISBN 978-1-62097-645-6 (ebook)

CIP DATA IS AVAILABLE

Book design and composition by Bookbright Media
This book was set in Minion and Kievit

Printed in the United States of America

10 9 8 7 6 5 4 3 2 1

Bottom row, left to right: Luz Vega-Marquis in the arms of her mother Susana Vega Solorzano, sister Claudia, father Octavio Vega Pasquier. Top row, left to right: brother Eduardo, cousin Elena, sister Belkys. Photo taken in Rivas, Nicaragua. *Photo courtesy of the author.*

To low-income families all over this country who are working toward a better life for themselves and their communities

To my dear family:

My loving parents and siblings. I was blessed to be born in Rivas, Nicaragua, an abode of love and the best town in the world

Dr. Bill Marquis, my soulmate and sweet husband, *mi amor*

Andres Vega, my rock and precious son, and Divina, my lovely daughter-in-law

My beautiful granddaughters—Amanda, Alynna, and Adriana—and my precious grandson Andres Bret, whose love keeps me young and who I pray will live in a safer, more just and loving world

Traveler, your footsteps are the road, and nothing more; traveler, there is no road, the road is made by walking.

Caminante, son tus huellas el camino, y nada más; caminante, no hay camino, se hace camino al andar.

—Antonio Machado

Contents

Foreword

DR. FREEMAN A. HRABOWSKI III

I first saw Luz in a hotel elevator, though I did not know who she was at the time. It was 2001, and the Marguerite Casey Foundation (MCF) board was holding one of its first meetings. The woman in the elevator impressed me as someone who was friendly and yet clearly on a mission. I could tell she was preparing for something important.

Several minutes later, as I sat in the board meeting, to my surprise, she entered the room and was introduced as Luz Vega-Marquis, a candidate for the foundation's CEO position. Although I had not met her in person before, we had studied her professional background and we had talked with her references. Everyone had said what we quickly found to be true: Luz understood our mission and was intensely committed to poor families. She brought impressive professional experience in philanthropy and demonstrated a deep understanding of what families of color and poor people experience in America every day. Shortly after that meeting, the board voted unanimously to invite her to lead the foundation. As impressive as she was, none of us could have imagined how transformative her visionary leadership would be.

Ask, Listen, Act weaves together two special stories. The first describes the journey of a Nicaraguan child who came to this country at the age of thirteen. Frightened, separated from her parents, she was unaware of the numerous challenges she would experience as a Latina immigrant growing up in America. She describes her experience sharing a bunk bed with five of her siblings, and she tells us what it was like having to leave her food desert neighborhood to walk to Safeway and back, struggling for two hours on the return trip carrying bags of groceries. One teacher told her she would fail in life. Another teacher believed in her and helped her attend college. All of these experiences, combined with a strong education, are at the center of her development as a leader. Luz understands the devastating impact of poverty on children and families. At the same time, she knows the importance of family. She has always found strength from her parents, siblings, and extended family and now her husband, children, and grandchildren. Family is at the center of her life.

The second story chronicles the evolution of a foundation, the crafting of its vision, and the development of a new model for philanthropy. In developing MCF's approach, Luz and her colleagues led a series of listening sessions in communities across the nation. The lessons they brought back from these sessions shaped our philosophy and strategies for working with families. That approach involves asking, listening, and then acting based on the experiences and voices of the families. Our belief in families and their ability to know what they need is at the core of the foundation's philosophy—understanding that supporting children means investing in families and attacking poverty.

The foundation has created a new narrative about poverty by developing a strong network of communities focused on policy change. Our organizing model encourages grantees to build networks to connect across race, ethnicity, geography, and class. Communities and low-income families are at the core of our work.

Over the years, Luz, her staff, our grantees, and the board have grown as thought partners focused on critical issues, learning, and policy. Our emphasis on listening carefully led to the critical decision to focus on movement building, with these families and selected community organizations—trusted institutions with deep roots in the communities they represent—serving as our experts. Listening to their voices helped us establish best practices, from providing general support to building a learning organization for grantees, foundation staff, and the board to creating Equal Voice Networks that bring grassroots activists and organizations together to find common ground and amplify their impact on policy at all levels. The foundation's success can be attributed in large part to its focus on supporting organizations that help families gain the skills they need to become powerful advocates for their children, including helping these families challenge systems when necessary. As the Equal Voice Networks have developed, families have witnessed numerous policy wins, from criminal justice reforms and higher wages to stronger education and health care policies.

Perhaps most importantly, this book shows how MCF, like its CEO, has benefited from a special rapport with grantees and families. For Luz and so many of us, the reality of what these families experience is deeply personal. The foundation's success comes from its authenticity. On the one hand, Luz and staff members have developed relationships with hundreds of organizations, from the Deep South to Chicago to California. MCF board members have benefited from substantive interactions with numerous community leaders and families because of these relationships. On the other hand, we learned to see the individual child. Every member of the staff and every board member knows the story of Joseph, a little boy whom board members met on one of our trips to Washington, D.C. Less than two years old and in the foster care system, he uttered no sounds and seemed to have no emotional ties. In many respects, he seemed lifeless. Luz never let us forget Joseph because he represented all those children who need the love of family.

At the beginning, fellow board members and I were, at best, cautiously optimistic that we could create a robust network of families across the country. However, we believed in Luz and her staff. Twenty years later, they have done the work we all envisioned. Now more than ever, this country needs strong, selfless leaders who listen to the voices of those who are too often ignored. This book gives us hope that America's children—including those from low-income and working families—can grow up to become inspiring leaders, that our foundations can empower families to lead, and that America can be better tomorrow than it is today.

Chapter 1: From the Beginning

None of us got where we are solely by pulling ourselves up by our bootstraps. We got here because somebody . . . bent down and helped us pick up our boots.

—Supreme Court Justice Thurgood Marshall

I stood on the stage at the Crystal City Marriott in Arlington, Virginia, listening to the hum of hundreds of conversations. As I waited to welcome the 450 people gathered for the 2018 Marguerite Casey Foundation (MCF) National Convening, I drew a quiet joy from watching attendees greet one another as old friends, exchanging pictures of children and grandchildren along with updates on their interwoven efforts to build a movement of poor and working families. Many were longtime MCF grantees as well as seasoned activists and veterans of successful campaigns to raise the minimum wage, improve access to child care, protect immigrant rights, and more. Several had told me that the gathering—which brought grantees and their constituents together with MCF staff and board members—felt more like a family reunion than a typical foundation convening.

After nearly two decades as founding president and CEO of the foundation, I suppose that makes me the matriarch. But in that moment before I turned on the microphone and began to speak, I was happy simply to be part of this remarkable community. Looking out at those assembled, I felt as if I were seeing a living panorama of the foundation's history. I saw old friends and new faces, longtime allies and young activists joining us for the first time. I saw MCF's history but also our future and drew comfort from the certainty that MCF's work would abide long after my own tenure had passed.

My journey to this place and this moment began with a missed phone call. It was July of 2001, and I was working as the head of the Community Technology Foundation in San Francisco. For the first time in years, my family and I had decided to take a vacation—the old-fashioned kind, before smartphones and Wi-Fi made it impossible to escape the buzz of the working world. I was determined to spend some much-needed time with my family and had promised them—and myself—that I would not even check my messages during our vacation. So while we enjoyed the blue waters of Maui, and each other's company, my answering machines at home and at work were filling up with calls about a job at a mysterious new foundation in Seattle.

By the time I got home and heard the messages, it was too late—the search committee had identified a candidate and closed the search. "Don't worry," I told Douglas Patiño, with whom I served on the board of the California Wellness Foundation and who was now on the board of this new foundation. "I like my job. I'm fine here."

I didn't give this missed opportunity much thought until several months later, when Douglas called again. The original hire had fallen through, and the committee had opened the search once again. It's not often that opportunity knocks twice, and when Douglas insisted that I apply, I figured I should pay attention. In October of 2001, I flew to West Palm Beach, where the board was meeting, for an interview. Before I flew home, I was handed a letter offering me the position.

There was much I did not know about this new foundation, but I sensed right away that I would be working with kindred spirits. Founding board members like Ruth Massinga, Douglas Patiño, Pat Schroeder, Freeman Hrabowski, and Bill Foege shared many of my values, most critically my deep commitment to families. Very quickly, it became clear to me that they could become both mentors and allies.

Nevertheless, the choice before me was not easy. I liked my job, and I have deep roots in the San Francisco Bay Area, where my son and his family and many of my extended family still live. But the board's passion was contagious, and the opportunity to be one of the architects of this new foundation was hard to resist. In the end, hope outweighed trepidation, and I accepted the job. Privately, I told myself I would give it five years—surely enough to put the foundation on strong footing—before returning to my beloved Bay Area. That was almost twenty years ago. This work has inspired and captivated me in ways I could barely begin to imagine when I began this journey.

Nothing else but family

When I reflect on how a thirteen-year-old immigrant who arrived in this country with one hundred dollars in her pocket grew up to lead a foundation that has invested close to half a billion dollars in building a movement of low-income families, my thoughts do not turn to a series of events or achievements. Instead, I see faces—the faces of key mentors and allies who believed in me over the years, who saw me not just for who I was at any particular moment but for who I might become. Throughout my life, I have been blessed with teachers, family members, and friends who, in the words of the great Supreme Court Justice Thurgood Marshall, bent down and helped me pull my boots up when I most needed a hand. Their faces form a sort of personal pantheon for me—a constant source of strength and inspiration. Each time I take a chance on a young, untested leader whose dreams exceed her resources, I am honoring those who took that chance on me.

I was thirteen years old when my family fled political turmoil in Nicaragua for the United States. Caught up in political tailwinds beyond my control, I spent my first year in this country at the home of a half-brother I barely knew, separated from my parents and most of my siblings. Bureaucratic issues and the size of my family—nine children in all—made it impossible for all of us to make the journey together, so I arrived here with one sister and one brother, unsure when I would see my parents again, if ever. I still remember how tightly I clung to my sister when the time came for us to go to separate classrooms at school. The truth is, we were terrified of losing one another. Perhaps as a result, we've remained so close that, to this day, we speak on the phone each morning before work.

Over the course of the following year, my family was gradually reunited in the United States. We were fortunate—we had documents that would allow us to live securely in the United States, and, most importantly, we had one another. But children are marked by their early experiences, and I carry the fear of separation with me to this day. When I look at the images of children being forcibly separated from their parents at the U.S.-Mexico border, I feel their pain in a visceral way. I don't pretend that our immigration circumstances were as dire as those so many families are facing today. But total change is hard, especially on children. And that is what it felt like to me as a child: in an instant, everything had changed, and I had no way of knowing whether anything would ever feel normal again.

I know firsthand what it is like to live with deep uncertainty. I know what it's like to feel totally lost—to feel invisible because I have no voice. These are feelings that never entirely go away. Painful as they are, these experiences shaped me to be a person who cares deeply about social justice. They not only inspire me to hold my own family close but also drive my work, fueling my commitment to all families who feel pushed to the outskirts of the American mainstream, whether by income, education, where they live, or where they come from.

My faith in family is what I rely on, what I value, and what I practice. The bottom line in my family is that we take care of one another. We may disagree, or even be in conflict, but I will help take care of you, and I know you will be there for me. This is how I was raised, and this is how my family functions to this day. It is also how MCF operates. When people ask me what personal values I bring to my work, I tell them that I am Latina, and family is it. There is nothing else for me but family. So perhaps it was inevitable that I would end up at a foundation that was not only committed to family but was itself the legacy of one remarkable family.

"How are the children doing?": The Casey family legacy

Long before there was a Marguerite Casey Foundation, there was the Casey family. That story begins in 1907, when Jim Casey, the oldest brother, launched a messenger service. This small family business would grow, over the years, into the United Parcel Service (UPS), a 58 billion-dollar business spanning several continents.

Although Jim Casey ultimately amassed great wealth, his early life left him intimately familiar with struggle. He left school in junior high in order to help his widowed mother, a seamstress, support him and his three siblings. At seventeen, he closed down his first messenger business in Seattle and set off for Nevada with a friend, hoping to prospect for gold. By the time they got there, the gold was gone, but Jim saw an opportunity to relaunch his messenger business in a rapidly growing town that had only a single telephone switchboard connecting thirty thousand residents. The business was just getting off its feet when his young partner was shot and killed while delivering a message. Then Jim himself came down with typhoid, which forced him to return home to Seattle, where he restarted his messenger business once again.

As UPS grew, so did the Casey family's commitment to philanthropy. In 1948, the four Casey siblings founded the Annie E. Casey Foundation, named in honor of their mother and charged with encouraging public policies, system reforms, and community supports to meet the needs of vulnerable children, youth, and families. In 1966, Jim Casey established Casey Family Programs (CFP), an operating foundation committed to improving foster care, in the family's hometown of Seattle. In 1976, the family established Casey Family Services to operate model foster care programs in Connecticut and Vermont. For the rest of his life, Jim Casey remained intimately involved in CFP's efforts, opening each board meeting with the same question: "How are the children doing?" When he died in 1983 at the age of ninety-five, he made a final bequest that expanded the family's support of disadvantaged children even further. This is the legacy into which MCF was born.

The foundation I was asked to lead was not initially known as the Marguerite Casey Foundation. At first, it was dubbed the Casey Family Grants Program, reflecting its close ties to CFP. In 2001, CFP launched the Casey Family Grants Program with a mandate to expand CFP's outreach and further enhance its thirty-seven-year record of leadership in child welfare. The new foundation would build on the philanthropic legacy of the Casey family, who had already invested millions in improving the lives of the most vulnerable children. As a first step, it would take CFP's work on foster care to the next level, deepening CFP's impact and enhancing its leadership in the child welfare arena and beyond.

The board and I were entrusted with an endowment of 600 million dollars—part of a larger sum that had been raised when the United Parcel Service went public in 1996—and a mandate to improve the lives of the nation's most vulnerable children and families. The initial mission—to promote best practices and partnerships that advance child welfare system reforms and projects that empower children, youth, and families to reach their full potential—was closely intertwined with that of CFP.

Jim Casey was a remarkable man. He lived his life and built his multibillion-dollar business guided by the belief, as he often said, that "the future of us all depends on how well we take care of one another." Today, this beautiful saying is etched on the glass wall of the MCF conference room so that we can remember and strive to live up to it. Jim Casey always attributed his company's success to the fact that he gave ownership of it to the people who did the work. He was a family man in the truest, most expansive sense of the word—his life revolved around taking care of his biological family as well as his employees, whom he viewed as his extended family.

His interest in foster care—and, more broadly, in supporting vulnerable youth—was sparked by his experience with the "messenger boys" who worked for him in the early days of UPS. Jim Casey made a point of getting to know each of the messengers personally. Many, he observed, came from fragile or troubled families. Lacking opportunity and family support, it was all too easy for some of these young people to drift into "mischief." He understood that this was not because they were bad kids but simply because they lacked the fundamental supports that had allowed him to prosper. Jim Casey made it his mission to ensure that young people grew up in supportive families, with ample opportunity to prosper and grow. Casey Family Programs—the manifestation of this mission—grew from a single site in Seattle to twenty-one sites in seventeen states over the course of twenty-five years.

Our first task was refining that mandate and defining the role and approach of this new philanthropic entity, starting with the name. If we were genuinely going to create something new, we needed a new name—one that honored our connection to the Casey family but also distinguished us from the various other foundations that carried the Casey name. I remember huddling with CFP President Ruth Massinga and Pat Schroeder—two of our founding board members—in a Washington, D.C., alley during a break at an early board meeting and discussing the possibility of naming the new foundation after Marguerite, the only woman among the Casey siblings. Born in Seattle in 1900,

Marguerite was the youngest of four children to Henry J. and Annie E. Casey. When Jim Casey launched CFP, he asked Marguerite to serve on the board, a post she accepted with enthusiasm. Like her brother Jim, Marguerite believed deeply in the importance of family and spent much of her adult life working to create opportunities for families and communities to thrive. When she died in 1987, Marguerite left the bulk of her fortune, approximately 650 million dollars, to CFP. Honoring Marguerite's life and work seemed the perfect way to launch this new endeavor. Her portrait holds a place of honor in our office to this day. Out of respect for one of the very few stipulations in her will, her portrait is always accompanied by fresh orchids.

Looking upstream

As we began the work of building a new philanthropy, the nation was embarking on a new millennium. It was a challenging time for poor and working families, who were finding it harder than ever to sustain themselves in the so-called "knowledge economy" of the twenty-first century. Poverty was rampant, unemployment was persistent, and many of the nation's schools were failing to meet even the most basic needs of their most vulnerable students. As the chasm been the "haves" and "have nots" widened, growing numbers of children—poor black and brown children in particular—were falling through the cracks. This is the juncture at which MCF was born.

The initial thinking was that the foundation would function as the corporate arm of CFP, making grants to advance CFP's pioneering work as an operating foundation. For decades, CFP had worked to improve outcomes for families involved with the child welfare system, establishing and running model programs in several states and regions. Despite CFP's best efforts, however, the flow of children into the system seemed inexorable. Those who left the system at the age of eighteen struggled with homelessness, joblessness, and incarceration. After decades of effort to improve the child welfare system, the time had come to turn toward a deeper question: what was causing the disruption, and often the permanent dissolution, of hundreds of thousands of families, and what would it take to keep those families together?

When I look back at this juncture in our institutional history, I think of a parable several grantees have shared over the years. There are a few variations on the story, but in each version, members of an unnamed village are alarmed to see a baby floating in the river. Needless to say, they jump in and rescue the struggling child, but the next day, it happens again. Soon the water is crowded with babies struggling to stay afloat, and it is all the villagers can do to save one before the next appears around the bend. Eventually, the crisis overwhelms their best efforts, and babies begin drowning before they can be saved.

Finally, one of the villagers breaks free of the group and begins to run along the path that leads up the mountain. "What are you doing?" cry the others. "Why aren't you staying to help save the babies?"

"I'm going upstream," he answers, "to find out who is throwing so many babies in the river and make it stop."

This was the mandate our nascent foundation took on: to go upstream, seek the source of the crisis that was manifesting as a flood of children into the foster care system, and do what we could to stem it at the source. As we wound our way upstream from the crisis that a child's removal from her family represents, we found a complex tangle of intersecting issues: a racially targeted War on Drugs; educational inequities; substandard housing; low-wage jobs that kept parents out of the home for long hours without paying enough to keep families afloat. Further upstream, these issues intersected in a single source: poverty. As the board and I reviewed the literature on children and families involved with the child welfare system, poverty emerged again and again as the single strongest risk factor for family separation. If we wanted children to thrive, we realized, we had to strengthen families. The only way to do that was to tackle poverty straight on.

From the beginning, we had a vision of the world we hoped to see—a world in which families were not forced apart simply because they did not have enough money. How to get there was the more difficult question. Our initial endowment of 600 million dollars allowed us to make 30 million dollars a year in grants. How could we best make use of these resources to tackle the immense problem of poverty in America? Our efforts to answer this question would set the course for this new foundation.

Standing up for all of us

As a child in Nicaragua, I studied English and French alongside my native Spanish, but sitting in a classroom did not prepare me for the overwhelming experience of making my way in a new country and a new language. I could read and understand English perfectly, but for several years after we came to the United States, I was afraid to open my mouth in public. This made the transition to high school challenging.

I still remember the first time I set foot on the campus of San

Francisco's Mission High School. The culture clash was incredible. In Nicaragua, I had been educated by nuns. I can still see myself as I was in my last class picture before we left for the United States, standing proudly in my heavy gabardine uniform with the big felt hat and crisp blue collar. This was a far cry from what I encountered in 1960s San Francisco. The freedom the young women had in the United States was hard for me to fathom. They stood right out in front of the school wearing shorts, smoking, hanging around with boys—this was not what I was used to seeing!

The boisterous energy of my classmates was intoxicating but also unnerving. I kept my head down and focused my energy on my studies. With my head in a book, I was on familiar ground. My father always made sure that his children studied, telling us that books were a way to open up new worlds. As a child in Nicaragua, I loved to read because it introduced me to places I'd never been, both real and imaginary. Later, as a teenage immigrant in the United States, I found myself *living* in a world that was new and unfamiliar. Books went from being an escape to something more practical—a field guide to this new environment.

Outside of books, my parents and siblings were my greatest teachers. To this day, the lessons I learned as a member of a tightly-knit immigrant family infuse every aspect of my life and work. Growing up as an immigrant teaches you to be very clear about who you are. You learn to protect your family at a young age because it often feels as if you are the only one who can. At the same time, because you learn to depend on a large circle of extended family, it teaches you that we are all connected.

My family had our struggles in the years after we arrived in the United States, but it never crossed our minds to seek help from outside sources. One of my younger sisters was so traumatized by the move that she refused to go to school. Where do you go for advice in this situation? We had no idea. If there were resources at the time that might have helped her address the trauma she had experienced, as well as adjust to a new school and a new country, we didn't know about them. All we knew was that skipping school was against the law, and that trouble with the law could divide our family again. So every day of her second-grade year, one of us walked her to school. She cried the whole way, but she made it through. That was how we did things: on our own, but always together.

The lessons I learned in my first years in this country have informed my work ever since—lessons about what it means to be poor, to be an immigrant, a person of color, as well as a member of a close and loving family. At one point, I remember six of us slept in the same bunk bed—three on the bottom, three on the top. Was that poverty? Yes, it was. It was also a big shift for us. In Nicaragua, my father was a lawyer. We were not millionaires, but we didn't have to worry about money. We had a big house, a television, and most of all, a sense of security.

When my father sent us to the United States ahead of him, he gave each child a hundred dollars. It was supposed to last a while, but in family folklore, I spent all my money—and my sister Nini's—on Bazooka bubble gum. The story doesn't add up—Bazooka cost five cents back then, and there's no way I could have chewed that much gum—but to this day, my sisters swear they found the wrappings under my bed.

We can laugh about it now, but money was a struggle in those first years after we arrived in the United States. Buying groceries, for example, was more than just a matter of figuring out how to pay for them. We lived in what today would be called a "food desert," and we didn't have a car, so my sisters and I would walk to the Safeway in another neighborhood. It took us two hours to get back carrying the heavy bags. Every few blocks, we would put them down to rest for a moment, then pick them up and keep on trudging until finally we reached home.

For a long time, home was the only place I felt free to be myself. Outside our door lay a strange new world where I was mindful to keep a low profile. Don't ask for too much, stay in your lane, don't cause any trouble—if you're an immigrant, this is how you survive. But I had a strong sense of justice, and there were times when keeping quiet was impossible for me, especially when I saw my family being mistreated. Doing errands with my mother when I was young gave me an early education in standing up to discrimination. We'd be standing in line somewhere waiting to pay, and the shopkeepers would consistently pass her by to wait on others. I'd say, "Wait a minute, she's been standing in line for ten minutes! Is her money not good enough?" To this day, I don't like to get loud—"Don't get my ugly out," I'll tell people—but if I witness or experience discrimination, you are going to hear from me.

The first time I walked into Bergdorf Goodman in New York, I remember, my knees were shaking. I could sense I was unwelcome, but I was not willing to be shut out because of my race. The young woman behind the makeup counter looked right past me as though I were invisible. "Do you work here?" I asked her politely. "I asked you for this lipstick and I want to pay for it. What exactly is the problem?" I got some dirty looks, but I also got the lipstick. I don't enjoy these petty confrontations, but when I stand up for myself, I'm standing up for my mother. When I stand up for her, I am standing up for all of us.

"Where there's rice and beans, everybody eats."

The most important thing I learned growing up in a tightly knit immigrant family is that family is the ultimate resource. No social service can match the support net provided by a family, no matter how economically stressed that family may be. And no one—not the government, not a public agency, and certainly not a distant foundation—knows better than that family what its members need.

The idea that families are more qualified than anyone else to articulate solutions to the challenges they face is central to the MCF ethos. At the same time, we understand that poor families need resources in order to have a shot at advancing those solutions. If you want to fight poverty, you must invest in families. In the long run, there is no investment that will pay off so richly.

There is a saying in my family: "Where there's rice and beans, everybody eats." Some in my extended family do not have much money, but we help one another, so no one is truly poor. That is social capital in action. Because families pool their resources, they provide the ultimate dividend on every dollar invested. Investing in families, I have learned from experience, is the best way to support children and to combat poverty. Children thrive when their families thrive: it really is that simple.

Why, then, do we so often ignore this basic truth, something we know from our own experience but routinely overlook when we talk about poor families? Why do we focus on an artificial

measure like "child poverty" when parents and children eat
from the same pot? The answer, I have come to believe, is that
too many of our anti-poverty efforts are rooted in the notion of
the "deserving poor." Rallying support for poor children is one
thing, because we can see them as "innocent victims." Their parents, on the other hand, are generally seen as the authors of their
own misfortune, unworthy of compassion, much less assistance.
This strikes me as the central fallacy about poverty: the notion
that income is a reflection of character. If there is one thing I
have learned from both personal and professional experience, it
is that poverty is a situation, not a characteristic.

My own experience growing up without much money taught
me valuable lessons about fiscal stewardship—lessons that apply
whether you are managing a 600-million-dollar endowment or
trying to make a paycheck stretch to the end of the month. When
you grow up, as my siblings and I did, putting paper in the soles
of your shoes to cover up the holes, you learn early on to watch
every penny. You also learn the value of a long-term investment.
My brothers still talk about the shoes my father made them wear
as teenagers—an age when sporting the right logo can feel like a
life-or-death matter. My brothers learned to dread the day when
their feet stopped growing. That's when my father would take
them out to buy a pair of shoes that, he promised (or threatened), they could wear for the rest of their lives. They were heavy,
clunky things, with thick rubber soles—the kind of shoes that
seem practical to an adult but feel like a social death sentence
to an adolescent. Maybe this experience is why I have so many
shoes to this day—not because I can't stop buying them, but
because I can't bring myself to throw a pair away.

The magic of a mentor

All through high school, I worked hard and tried to keep my head down. I didn't think much about where my studies might take me after high school simply because I didn't know what opportunities existed. My greatest hope was that I might find my way to community college. I didn't know there was more out there and neither did my parents. There was no counseling at the school I attended. My dreams were conscribed by my limited knowledge.

As an immigrant and a Latina, I learned early on that I would have to fight to belong. At Mission High, I was a good student and a hard worker, and while this attracted the caring attention of some of my teachers, it evoked a surprising hostility from others. I remember walking out of an assembly where I had been recognized for winning two small scholarships. When my homeroom teacher pulled me aside, it was not to congratulate me. "Don't get so cocky that you think you're going to make it," he told me scornfully. "You're going to fail, just like everybody else here."

It wasn't the first or last time I'd get this kind of message, but kids don't forget this kind of experience. To this day, I can see this man's face in front of me. But as soon as I do, his sneering voice is drowned out by my father's gentler tones. "Don't pay attention to him," my father told me when I came home from school distraught over my teacher's words. "This man doesn't know you. He doesn't know your family. He doesn't know where you come from. He doesn't know that we all believe in you."

I can still see my father as he was in those early years when we were trying to gain a foothold in this country. His law degree was not valid in the United States, so he went to San Francisco State University and studied for a new career as a Spanish teacher. I can see him now in his brightly colored shirts and ties, with his long mustache and wild fringe of hair (he didn't have much hair left by that time, but what little bit he had, he was determined to wear long). I was very close to him and to my mother. My parents were supportive of all their children, regardless of what we did with our lives.

I also had the good fortune to meet people like Mrs. Burchard, my U.S. history teacher. Mrs. Burchard was a tiny, big-hearted Mexican American woman who saw something in seventeen-year-old me that I had not yet fully recognized in myself—a spark of ambition that, like all great teachers, she was determined to fan into a flame. If she had not believed in me and gone out of her way to help me, there is no way I would be where I am today. I owe her my life because I owe her my education.

One day, Mrs. Burchard asked me where I was planning to go to college. When I told her my hope was to go to the nearest two-year school, she was uncharacteristically stern. "Absolutely not," she said firmly. "You can do better."

After class the next day, Mrs. Burchard handed me an application to the University of San Francisco (USF), a competitive private school that I had never heard of, despite the fact that it was just a few miles from my home. As I scanned the application, my heart began to beat faster. Then I read the small print: just applying to this school required a fifty-dollar fee. My family didn't have fifty dollars to spare. "I can't do it," I told Mrs. Burchard. "I can't apply."

"I will pay it," she responded in that teacherly tone that lets you know the subject is no longer up for discussion. To this day, when I hear talk of "leveraging resources," I think of the investment Mrs. Burchard made in me. I never got a chance to ask her what it was she saw in me that made her take that chance, but I do know that I am here today because of her. That fifty dollars— and the vote of confidence that it represented—changed the course of my life.

I enrolled at USF the fall after I graduated from high school. USF could not have been more different from Mission High. I went from a crowded, underfunded public high school to the lush, verdant campus of a selective Jesuit university where students from wealthy families spent several times my family's annual income on a year's tuition. I chose to study accounting, not because I had a passion for the subject but because I needed a good job to help support my family. That's what I was looking for from a college education.

USF is a wonderful school, and from my first day on campus I felt blessed to be there. At the same time, I always felt like a fish out of water. Most of my classmates came from well-to-do families. They spoke casually of their ski trips, their summer vacations, and the cars their parents bought them as graduation presents. I rode the bus and spent my vacations working extra hours to pay for books and other expenses that my scholarship didn't cover.

I could handle the academics, but the class gap made the social aspect difficult. It was hard to relate to the casual entitlement I saw around me. But this too became part of my education. Holding my own in a place that was foreign and not always friendly was valuable training for a career in philanthropy.

A crash course in philanthropy

Because I was an accounting major with a knack for numbers, USF assigned me to a work-study job in the bursar's office. The James Irvine Foundation was a major donor to higher education at that time, and I kept seeing checks come in under their name. Soon, I was tracking all of the expenses associated with the Irvine Foundation's grants to USF. Eventually, the Irvine Foundation offered me a job as a bookkeeper. I still remember my first visit to their office at 111 Sutter Street in San Francisco with the sleek leather couches and the huge boardroom with its glossy conference table. The sums of money that passed through this institution, the kind of power that represented—all of it was mind-boggling.

I switched to evening classes and began spending my days at Irvine's downtown office. By the time I turned twenty-two, I was working full-time at the Irvine Foundation while taking a full load of courses at USF. I stayed there for the next seventeen years, moving up from bookkeeper to program officer to director of grants. The education I got at Irvine was as important as the one I received at USF, because it was there that I discovered the power of philanthropy to seed social change. I also learned how to push boundaries, sometimes openly, sometimes subtly. I was always looking for ways to stretch the work of the foundation and expand our impact into the most underserved and overlooked communities—those like the one where I came of age.

Looking back, I am amazed at how young I was when I began my career in philanthropy. It was the sixties, and I would wear the styles of the day—miniskirts and knee-high boots—with my own personal spin. Every morning when I did my makeup, I would paint a heart on my face with a black Maybelline eyebrow pencil and then fill it in with red lipstick, something I had seen on a movie poster from Mexico. Wearing my heart on my face, so to speak, was my tiny sign of rebellion: "This is who I am. Take it or leave it."

Meanwhile, I did everything I could to prove myself through my work. At the beginning, my responsibilities were limited to bookkeeping, so I set about being the best bookkeeper the foundation had ever seen. I remember when I got there, they had all the grants they had ever made on three-by-five-inch index cards. No one had ever reconciled these cards with the general ledger. I reconciled it all by hand, coming back after my classes at USF and working late into the night. Later, I typed grant write-ups on an IBM Selectric typewriter, painstakingly lining up bits of correction film until each document was error-free. My boss was extremely particular about this kind of thing—down to the staple, which had to be applied vertically, not horizontally—and I was determined to rise to the challenge. My years at Irvine fueled a perfectionism that has stayed with me to this day. It has served me well on the numerous occasions where people question my competence before they know a thing about me beyond my race and gender.

I learned a tremendous amount in my years at the Irvine Foundation. I remember receiving a proposal from Equal Rights Advocates (ERA) for an initiative on sexual harassment in the workplace. As a young woman trying to make my way in the professional world, I understood all too well that the work they were proposing was essential. I also knew that the male-dominated board was not going to approve the grant—it was 1980, and sexual harassment was not yet on the national radar. I

decided my best bet was to be upfront. I told the executive director of ERA that I was willing to present the proposal if they were
willing to have it denied. I presented it to her exactly as I saw
it: an opportunity for the board to be exposed to the reality of
what was happening to women in the workplace and to the idea
that there were people out there trying to do something about
it. She thanked me for being honest and submitted a proposal,
knowing full well that it would not be funded. Sure enough, the
board turned it down, but at least we had gotten the issue on
their radar. I could see it in their faces as I presented the grant:
they were beginning to think about something in a new way.
After this, every time the board met I would bring one organization before them that was not in the traditional mold of the
foundation. Over time, the idea of funding social change became
less threatening to them.

In some ways, the Irvine Foundation was like USF all over
again. The most difficult part was the social hour with the
board. I could handle my work, but talking about bird watching? The class difference was incredible! Navigating that chasm
was another valuable skill I developed during those early years.
When I look at myself now, it's hard to believe I was once a
shaky-voiced young woman whose heart nearly pounded out of
my chest whenever I had to stand up in front of people and present a grant, much less express an opinion.

Class was not the only thing that set me apart from my colleagues in philanthropy. I quickly grew accustomed to being the
only non-white person in the room, but it took some a while to
get used to me. Long after I had been promoted to a program
officer position, visitors would hand me their coats when they
walked into a meeting or ask me to get them a cup of coffee.

Later on, as I got to know other people of color working in philanthropy, I would hear similar stories again and again.

Feeling like an outsider did not stop me from learning everything I could during my years at the Irvine Foundation, or from finding valuable mentors along the way. These early experiences are the fire in which my values were forged. The lessons I drew from my family and our shared experience as immigrants to America, and later from key teachers and mentors who guided me, have shaped my life and my values. But how do you make your values manifest in the world? This would be the challenge of the next two decades.

Chapter 2: A Learning Journey

I've never met a family that doesn't know what it needs. They know what they need.

—*Listening Circle participant, Mobile, Alabama*

In early 2002, the Marguerite Casey Foundation began operations in our new office on Dexter Street in Seattle. Mindful of our commitment to keep overhead low and conserve our resources for grantmaking, we did not indulge in the costly renovations that often mark the launch of a new foundation, but we did enjoy decorating the office to reflect the rich mix of cultures and backgrounds our staff and grantees represent. From Native American paintings to African baskets, the office was a visual celebration of peoples and cultures.

With the help of Casey Family Programs (CFP) and other partners nationwide, we designed a research program to identify the areas where our grant dollars could have the greatest impact. We began by commissioning forty "thinking papers" from researchers and practitioners in the fields of child welfare and family well-being. We conducted dozens of interviews with practitioners; fellow grantmakers; and pioneers from the battles for civil rights, voting rights, immigrant rights, environmental justice, fair housing, a livable wage, Indian sovereignty, child welfare reform, and more. We surveyed the literature and demographics of the field. Later, we would take what we had learned back to the community, holding Listening Circles with more than six hundred community members in six sites across the nation.

"What would you do with 30 million dollars a year in grant-making funds?" we asked the individuals we approached with requests for thinking papers. We weren't interested in short-term initiatives, we told them. We were looking for lasting, community-generated solutions to long-term problems and divisions. We reached out to researchers and academics, but we also invited papers from those doing the work on the ground. Most importantly, we went directly to families themselves. While our initial mandate was relatively narrow—to discover what it would take to stem the flow of children into foster care—the more deeply we looked, the broader our scope became. Again and again, the thinking papers brought home to us that poverty, along with racial bias, was the prime driver behind foster care placement. Beneath these core drivers were layer upon layer of complexity. We learned about the challenges confronting the many families who face the twin demons of racism and poverty. The more we learned, the more complex we understood our challenge to be.

At the same time, a powerful current of hope ran through the papers we received. We were moved by the collective energy we saw brewing within and among diverse communities—the connections they were already making with one another. In Oakland, for example, Asian Immigrant Women Advocates was bringing together low-income immigrant Latina and Asian women who worked in the restaurant, garment, and electronics industries to learn from one another's struggles and successes.

Whether they came from China, Korea or Mexico, these women all shared the experience of struggling to find a foothold in a new country with limited English and few marketable skills. Even in the face of the most daunting challenges, these women and others like them were leading successful campaigns to shorten workdays, increase wages, and improve unhealthy or dangerous working conditions. Together, they had marshalled a strength that, on their own, would have been out of reach.

Through education and leadership development, we came to see, members of the nation's poorest communities could improve not only their own lives but those of their families and neighborhoods. Ultimately, working in coalition with other similarly situated groups, they could change policy at the local, state, and even federal levels. As one immigrant activist put it, "everyday people can make the government change, but you have to work hard, and you have to do it together."

Again and again, the authors of the thinking papers urged us to move beyond the individualism that characterizes so much of the political discourse in America; to situate child well-being in the context of family and community; and, crucially, to amplify the voices and bolster the collective power of families. "Much of the grantmaking that is done in low and moderate-income communities is done 'for' people instead of 'with' people," wrote noted economist Julianne Malveaux. "It seems to me that the voices of the people whose life you want to improve are invaluable as you embark on this process."

The simple act of speaking out, we learned, could turn a vicious cycle into a positive one. By joining together in raising their voices, newly hatched activists could begin to change the conditions that held them and their families back. With each small victory, their courage grew, and with it their collective power. Mothers and fathers became organizers, peer counselors, advocates, and activists. Their brave efforts bolstered our own commitment to supporting grassroots leadership in all of our endeavors.

The more we learned about this kind of collective effort, the more determined we became not only to support it but to make it a centerpiece of our grantmaking ethos. Families were vulnerable, we learned, but together they were powerful. If we wanted to tap into this power, families and their community leaders needed to be at the center. It wasn't enough to ask community residents to show up at public hearings and meetings but not be part of the planning and decision-making processes. Families themselves needed to be in leadership roles when decisions were made about them. As one young activist put it, "We don't want just a seat at the table. We want to be the ones who are writing the menu."

This was not the standard approach. More typically, funders set their own priorities and then seek grantees who can help to achieve them. We wanted to turn that top-down approach on its head. Out of this grew our brand promise: "Ask, Listen, Act." Our priorities would not be set in the boardroom, nor our own offices. Before we took a single step, we would *ask* the families we aimed to serve what they most needed in order to determine the course of their own lives. We would *listen* closely to what they told us, because their analysis would undergird all of our activities moving forward. Only when we had a clear sense of what families needed and wanted would we *act* in support of their efforts. To this day, our "Ask, Listen, Act" philosophy guides every aspect of our work, inspiring us constantly to challenge conventional thinking, starting with our own.

Listening Circles

As the tiny eight-seat airplane began the descent into Yakima, Washington, my mind replayed the hundreds of conversations that had made the past six weeks so rich and revealing. Months earlier, on September 11, 2001, the Twin Towers had fallen in New York, sending the country into a tailspin of fear and mutual suspicion. It was a difficult time for the endeavor we had taken on—a series of frank, community-level conversations about what families needed—but we had been met with an openness and enthusiasm that offered a powerful antidote to the anger and divisiveness that marked the national discourse.

The thinking papers had served as a springboard to phase two of our investigation: a series of Listening Circles that brought us into direct communication with those we aimed to support. If we were going to address poverty, we were determined poor people needed to be in the room. This simple conviction undergirded the entire planning process for what would become the Marguerite Casey Foundation. So in this second phase, we took our questions on the road, traveling to six regions in the country where family poverty was especially acute in order to engage directly with local families and community leaders. Yakima would be the last of these gatherings.

The Listening Circle draws on the American town hall and similar traditions from various cultures. Whether it is African elders gathering under the baobab tree, Native Americans coming together in a talking circle, or Latino communities joined in a lively *encuentro*, these gatherings provide a venue not only for the debate of issues but also for the opening of hearts. Our hope in hosting these initial sessions was to create a space—rare in the funding world—where nothing was taboo and everything was open to discussion. We sought, through these conversations, to deepen both the impact and the authenticity of our grantmaking practice.

Over the course of six intense weeks, we traveled to Los Angeles, California; Baltimore, Maryland; Mobile, Alabama; Rapid City, South Dakota; El Paso, Texas; and Yakima, Washington. We heard from family members, state and city officials, community and religious leaders, business representatives, public agency staff, young people and elders, as well as leaders of an array of innovative programs and organizations. In Mobile, participants traveled from Louisiana, Mississippi, and Tennessee to join the conversation. In Rapid City and Yakima, members of Native American tribes journeyed for hours to listen and be heard.

The Listening Circles were a traveling celebration of the American family in all of its glorious diversity. We met families who lived in remote rural outposts and others who made their homes in the heart of the nation's cities; families of every possible racial and ethnic composition; native-born and immigrant; LGBTQ and straight; biological, adoptive, and foster. In each city, participants shared a wide range of perspectives on what family meant to them—views that were shaped by cultural heritage, tradition, language, and more. It quickly became clear that conventional notions of family were not only outdated but entirely inadequate to describe the array of relationships that bind people together. Families, we heard again and again, are complex and changing entities that include, but also extend beyond, biological ties.

Much of the foundation's work to this day is rooted in what we heard during those early gatherings. The people who attended came from various neighborhoods and cultures. They represented multiple sectors and systems, varying ages and ethnicities, and divergent political perspectives. Yet when it came to the most important issues in their lives, common themes consistently emerged. The families we spoke with all sought a safe place where they could raise their children. They wanted jobs that paid a living wage so they could support those families and were willing to work hard at those jobs once they found them. They wanted access to health care for themselves and their children, and education that would give their children a shot at reaching their own dreams.

The circle widens

The more I listened to families themselves speak not only of their struggles but also of the deep bonds that sustained them, the more convinced I became that this new foundation had to go beyond the foster care system and tackle the root causes of family separation. Trying to fix the system felt like what we used to call a *rompe cabeza*, or head buster—those frustrating little plastic puzzles where you move the squares around trying to make them fit together, with every solution creating a new problem. If we wanted to make things better for children, we had to get outside the square of the system and think deeply about what it was they really needed. When we did, the answer always came down to the same thing: what children need is families.

For children to thrive, their families must also thrive. For families to flourish, communities also must flourish. The more we heard, the clearer this became. Our central mandate—helping children thrive and reach their full potential—never wavered, but our sense of how best to approach that mandate was profoundly shaped by what we heard from those six hundred voices on our listening tour.

I will never forget what I heard during the six weeks we travelled from one Listening Circle to the next. I learned what families needed and what they had to offer, but more than that, I learned who families *were*. That experience was the bedrock on which MCF was built.

From bustling downtown Los Angeles to sultry summertime Mobile and every Listening Circle city in between, MCF staff and board members heard diverse voices—some shouting, others whispering, all deeply engaged with the question of how change happens. While the unique circumstances of each region contributed to the breadth of perspectives gathered, these six hundred voices spoke with an astounding consistency. Together, Listening Circle participants called for a body politic that respected families—for public agencies that valued families and held them at the center of systems of care. They wanted to see more support for grassroots activism and leadership; better collaboration across agencies and systems; changes to policies that were unresponsive to families' voices and needs; and a strengthened public will to support families in ways that would avert the separation of parents and children. These values became linchpins of MCF's grantmaking practice over the years that followed, underscoring our commitment to "Ask, Listen, Act."

Listening Circle participants applauded the foundation's commitment to invest 30 million dollars annually in grants that strengthen families and communities, with an explicit emphasis on the needs of families in poor communities. We have maintained this central commitment ever since. Participants stressed the need to include families whose needs are often overlooked by major funders: those in Native American communities; ethnically diverse border communities; and rural communities, especially those in Southern states. These communities are represented in our grantmaking regions to this day. Attendees asked the foundation to strengthen the infrastructure within communities by investing in grassroots, neighborhood-based efforts, including the informal networks of support that are often closest to families but tend to be overlooked for funding. Support for grassroots organizing is at the heart of our ongoing work. Social movements, participants told us, rarely succeed unless they have strong mechanisms to identify, engage, and train new generations of leaders. The foundation consistently prioritizes supporting emerging leaders.

Participants asked us to help connect them to one another by investing in local, regional, and national networks. Network building is central to MCF's practice—so much so that we now require grantees to use networks to collaborate via seventeen robust networks across the country. Noting that popular media often neglects or negatively portrays families in under-resourced communities, attendees asked us to help amplify community voices. This mandate is central to MCF's communications strategy.

We asked challenging questions and listened carefully to every word and idea expressed. What emerged from this process could not have been clearer: the foundation needed to focus on the complex set of challenges facing low-income families. At the same time, we needed to help them strengthen their own voices and mobilize their communities in order to effect lasting systemic and social change. The idea that came through most clearly throughout was the value of focusing on movement building—and through that, empowering families—rather than simply providing direct services. You cannot service people out of poverty, our constituents told us again and again. They were looking for deeper, structural change. What they sought from us were tools. They would do the rest.

As a result of what we learned in those first months of listening, the board and I made a commitment that guides our efforts to this day. That commitment went beyond the traditional "issue areas" to encompass a central strategy: *In all of our efforts as a foundation, we will work to advance movement building among low-income families, grounded in the understanding that families are the experts on their own lives.*

We had asked. We had listened. Now it was time to act.

Chapter 3: Family-Centered Grantmaking

Don't judge each day by the harvest you reap but by the seeds that you plant.

—*Robert Louis Stevenson*

When the Marguerite Casey Foundation first went public with the idea of building a family-led movement, there were many who saw us as outliers. "Why families?" we were asked again and again. There are strategic reasons for organizing our grantmaking around the unit of the family. But the truth is, the impulse to focus our energy on families—and to capitalize on the energy families generate themselves—is also a deeply personal one for me. I am a sister to eight siblings and *una tía* to their children. I am a wife, a mother, a daughter. I am *una abuela* to six wonderful grandchildren. All of this is central not only to my life but to my sense of what matters. I place my faith in the family structure, whatever structure a particular family may take.

The MCF board was introduced to this aspect of who I am the moment they offered me the job. My husband Bill and I had flown out to West Palm Beach for an interview. Within a few hours of that conversation, the board offered me the job. It was so clearly the perfect opportunity for me that I think they were surprised by my initial response. "I'll have to get back to you," I told them. "I need to talk to my family."

"What do you mean?" one of the board members asked me. "Your husband is right here—you can talk to him now."

"No," I told them, "you don't understand. I have 120 people I need to go talk to."

It may seem hard to believe, but I was not exaggerating. For me, as a Latina, the concept of an extended family has always been a given. When I talk about my family, I am talking not only about children and grandchildren and siblings but also aunts, uncles, cousins, and more—a densely woven web spread across the San Francisco Bay Area.

When I came home and began telling my family about the remarkable opportunity I'd been offered to lead this new foundation, they were all thrilled for me. Then I told them the job was in Seattle, 800 miles away. From the strength of their reaction, it might as well have been on another planet. "You can't leave!" one of my younger sisters exclaimed. "We *came* here together. We have to stay together."

We talked and talked and talked, and eventually, my family came to understand that I was talking about leaving San Francisco, not about leaving *them*. We would still be in the same time zone; we could talk every day. I gave my grandchildren a map with a circle around Seattle and promised I'd be back to visit them every two weeks. They were too young to understand what "two weeks" meant, so I gave them a calendar and showed them how to mark off the days. Eventually, together, my family and I made the decision: it would be hard, but the opportunity to make a difference outweighed that personal hardship. I took the job, packed up the apartment, and set off with Bill for the drive to Seattle.

Remembering Joseph

Initially, our new foundation was closely bound up with Casey Family Programs, and our first grants were continuations of their long effort to improve the lives of children in foster care. As I began to explore this terrain, I was acutely aware of what it meant for children to be separated from their families. I had experienced that separation myself when I came to this country ahead of my parents and most of my siblings, and now, as an adult, I was experiencing it again. But none of this prepared me for meeting a little boy named Joseph. I encountered him only briefly, but this lonesome child made an indelible impression, cementing my commitment to building a foundation that would honor and protect the bonds of family.

We were in Washington, D.C., to meet with a group that had received a large grant to support its work improving foster care. This group practiced a form of collaborative case management that brought together birth parents, foster parents, and the various professionals involved in a child's life to share information and plan together for each child's future. The meeting we sat in on revolved around a child named Joseph. Not yet two years old, Joseph had already been in multiple placements. As I watched him, I was stunned by his utter passivity. As the many adults involved in Joseph's care discussed how best to meet his needs, the child himself was passed from one person to the next. Joseph appeared emotionless, neither clinging nor recoiling no matter whose lap he landed in, never uttering a sound. Looking at this child who seemed to have no emotional connection to any of the adults in his life, it was all I could do not to weep. I thought of my own young granddaughter, who clung to a parent's leg whenever a stranger was near. Joseph was not even two years old, yet he had already developed coping mechanisms in response to being passed from one home to another. As the case management team earnestly discussed Joseph's various needs, the collective silence around his most basic need—a child's need for secure attachment—was deafening. The visit where I met Joseph has stayed in my mind ever since, a haunting reminder of what can happen when a child's physical needs are met but his primal need for emotional connection—for *family*—is not.

MCF's stated commitment at that time included ensuring that children reached their full potential. By that measure, we were not doing well by Joseph. I held my tongue in the moment, but I made a silent promise to Joseph that day: to look at all of MCF's efforts through his young eyes and to do better by him and all the children like him.

When the MCF board next met, I spoke of how painful it had been to sit through this well-intentioned meeting. What, I challenged the board and myself, were our aspirations for a child like Joseph? Someone responded by pointing out that the material needs of the children in the care of this particular agency were being well met. They slept in clean beds and ate healthy food. A roof over your head and three meals a day? This was not enough to want for any child. Joseph may have had care, but what he needed was love—the consistent, hands-on love that all children need to thrive. We had to do better by children like Joseph, and that meant more than providing improved foster care services.

Remembering the detachment I saw in his eyes, and thinking about the lack of connection it reflected, strengthened my determination to move our work upstream—to focus our grantmaking on creating a world where children could thrive *alongside* their parents rather than being forced to undergo the trauma of separation in order to get their basic material needs met.

When I met Joseph, it struck me that what went unsaid was as important as what was said. Yes, there was a sincere effort to figure out what services and supports Joseph needed now that he had been separated from his family. But why were so many black and brown children being separated from their families in the first place? The child welfare system gives the government tremendous power over poor families—some of it warranted but much of it not. Conventional wisdom is that children in foster care are all the victims of terrible abuse. Some are, and in those cases, removal from their families constitutes a necessary rescue. But too often, kids are taken from their families because those families are poor. Poverty may be described in terms of "neglect," but I have met very few parents over the years who would intentionally choose to neglect their children. Neglect charges can come about when parents can't afford child care and are forced to leave children in the care of siblings while they work multiple jobs to support the family. They may be triggered when parents cannot afford medical care, food, or clothing, and children show up at school hungry with holes in their shoes. If you asked these children what they would rather have, new shoes or the parents who loved them, I think we all know what the answer would be. But no one asks the children. Instead, the machine grinds on, driven by its own imperatives, with families, too often, as the casualty. Having grown up in a family that meant more to me than anything, a family that at times was affected by poverty, this was a cycle I was determined to avert. Meeting Joseph broke my heart, but it also deepened my conviction that the most powerful thing our new foundation could do for children was to support their families and strengthen family voices.

MCF's commitment to family-centered grantmaking is grounded in strategy but also in simple common sense. We know that children are not poor because of their own inability to find gainful employment. They are not malnourished or undereducated by their own choosing, nor do they have control over where they live and what resources they can access. Instead, their lives are shaped by economic realities that keep their families, and their communities as a whole, under duress and disconnected from opportunities for success. If we want to improve children's prospects, we have to tackle the larger constellation of concerns that affect their families.

As MCF evolved, this determination to view the child as part of a larger family system rather than as an independent entity came to inform all of our work. It formed the basis for our efforts to develop a new cadre of parents and youth as civic leaders. It was the driver behind our commitment to investing in family-friendly models of community organizing. Above all, it was the impetus for seeking out organizations that were growing an organized base of families.

In order to create lasting change in children's lives, we had to support parents and caregivers in becoming informed and engaged advocates capable of navigating—and, when necessary, challenging—multiple systems in order to improve the lives of their families. When families *are* supported and given the opportunity to be heard on the issues that shape their lives, individual needs get met and social problems are prevented.

Building a family-centered philanthropy

"Family" has become such a politicized term in this country that I feel compelled to define what I mean when I use the word. When I say "family," I don't necessarily mean two married parents, 2.3 children, and a cute little dog. I am talking about a mutually supportive structure in which children are cared for by loving adults.

Investing in this structure makes sense to me as a philanthropist and even as a bookkeeper, because I have yet to encounter an entity that can stretch a dollar as skillfully as a family. When whatever is available goes into a single pot, no one goes hungry and no one is left behind. The family structure is powerful because it is expressly designed for the purpose of caring for one another. Ultimately, that is also the purpose of philanthropy. The word "philanthropy" means "for the love of mankind." At MCF that translates as "for the love of families." Families, in turn, love their kids, their communities—whatever makes up their sphere of influence. Maximizing the social and political power of this love drives everything we do.

Maybe this is why I was so surprised by the questions and comments I got when MCF went public with our commitment to family-centered grantmaking. "Isn't that the purview of the right wing?" people asked. "How are you going to organize them?" The underlying assumption was that families who lived in poverty were doomed to a state of powerlessness. But I knew differently. I knew it from our research but also in my heart: there is no force on earth as powerful as the love that binds a family. If MCF could find a way to harness that power, there was nothing I could not imagine us achieving.

We have always aimed to be strategic in our grantmaking, but we want that strategy to come from the ground up—to be designed and implemented by the families most affected. That means operating from the premise that the families who are closest to the problems of poverty are also closest to the solutions. From the start, these families have been our true constituency. We are answerable to them above all else.

At the same time, MCF has always considered itself a learning organization, and the learning did not stop when the grantmaking began. As our first docket approached, we accelerated our efforts to learn from colleagues, families, and potential grantees, scouring the country for organizations that shared our values and sense of mission. By necessity, our grants would go to organizations rather than to individual families, but our ultimate goal was not to create better organizations—it was to help build stronger families. With this in mind, I insisted that our travels take us not only inside nonprofit organizations but into the living rooms and kitchens of families themselves. Nearly twenty years later, these encounters remain vivid in my memory.

I will never forget visiting the Rio Grande Valley in 115-degree heat to meet with families living in the *colonias* on the U.S. side of the border with Mexico. Average family income in the *colonias* was 4,500 dollars a year. As many as half a million people were living in these massive slums, most without water or sewage service and many without access even to paved roads.

When I learned that local families, many of whom were Mexican immigrants, were losing their children because they lived in dilapidated homes they did not have the money to fix, I was heartbroken and angry. How were these parents supposed to become better providers when they did not have access to jobs that paid a living wage? These were not the "lazy" parents of stereotype and myth—they worked harder than just about anyone I knew. But in the absence of living-wage jobs, they were forced to cobble together a living from part-time work and small businesses they built from the ground up. What they had achieved was impressive, but no matter how hard they worked, it wasn't enough to pull their families out of poverty.

In McAllen, Texas, I met a woman whose children had been taken because Child Protective Services (CPS) thought the crowded, immaculate hand-built shack she lived in was "not good enough" to raise a family. Her children slept close together in a single room, a situation CPS deemed unacceptable. I thought of my own family during our most difficult years, when we had just arrived in this country and were struggling to get our footing. What if CPS had knocked on our door and seen six of us sleeping in a single bunk bed because that was all we could afford at the time? Would they have determined that my parents' heroic efforts were "not good enough"? Would they have taken me and my siblings away, separating me from the people I loved most? If that had happened, I cannot imagine how my life would have unfolded or who I would be today.

What I remember about those early years in the United States is not the number of square feet I was able to call my own—it's the late-night conversations I shared with my sisters as we went to sleep, close together enough to hear each other's whispers. Luckily, no one was measuring the square footage of our bedroom to determine whether we met their standards as a family. As I sat in that tiny home in McAllen, listening to a heartbroken mother grieve for her lost children, I remembered my own childhood and made a silent promise: to commit the resources of our young foundation to strengthening families and amplifying their voices so that no child would be separated from his parents simply because they were poor.

"The poor must talk to the poor"

That early visit to the *colonias*—the first of many to follow—was at once heartbreaking and inspiring. The depth of the poverty in which families were living took my breath away, but so did the strength of their commitment to one another. *That*, it struck me, was a great untapped resource. Families, in MCF's vision, are the fulcrum from which change can occur. When we talk about movement building at MCF, we are always talking about organizing families.

In West Texas, I braced myself against the wind that swept across the pit where Carlos Jacobo stomped mud and straw to make adobe bricks. The wind was relentless, rattling the tar paper on his old shack and lifting the blue cotton curtains his wife had carefully hung in their half-finished home. Saplings planted outside the door bent almost to snapping. Finally, the wind died down, providing a quiet interlude for Barbara Jacobo to tell me about the day, seven years earlier, when her new husband brought her to the patch of land where they would make their home. "I told myself then, 'I just gotta survive,'" she said. Surviving in the *colonias* meant living without electricity or running water. It meant using an outhouse. Worst of all, she said, it meant being invisible.

Initially, Carlos, a welder disabled by a work accident, was embarrassed to bring Barbara to this *colonia* in the desert east of El Paso, one of hundreds in a belt of substandard subdivisions that peppered the state's border with Mexico. Residents had bought land from often-unscrupulous developers who promised services in a future that never came. Over the years she and her husband had spent here, Barbara had adjusted to bathing out of five-gallon buckets, and when there was no fuel for their camp stove, to cooking with wood in a sawed-off barrel. She got used to driving fifty miles to work at a Walmart, switching to the overnight shift because it paid fifty cents more an hour. Carlos, meanwhile, spent his days making adobe bricks by hand and slowly building their house, which had grown to two fine, solid rooms by the time we visited.

"They never told me it wouldn't have water," Carlos said of the two acres he bought in 1984. This *colonia*, called Villa Alegre, was five times as big as the nearest town, Fort Hancock, yet its streets remained nameless. It didn't appear on any map. Because it had not been properly zoned for residential use, it was ineligible for county water. An electric pump could have run water from a tank into the Jacobos' house, but in a sinister Catch-22, the law said electricity could not be provided to places that did not already have water service.

"It's unjust," Carlos said. "If we're paying taxes, why must we live without light? They don't listen."

Most *colonia* residents are Mexican American or immigrants from Mexico, bringing the connection between poverty and

racism into stark relief. In a *colonia* called Asención, Miguel
Guzman, a convenience store clerk and father of three, put it this
way: "It feels like there is one constitution for America, and for
us here, another kind of law." Miguel's home was dotted with
tiny dishes of pancake syrup and vinegar, a potion to keep away
green flies from nearby dairy operations. Health clinics were a
mere dream. Mothers with sick kids went to a certain neighbor
because she had a phone and could call the emergency line at an
El Paso hospital fifty-five miles away. "They tell me to check for
fever or see whether the child can bend his head, and they tell me
what he needs, or to call the ambulance," said the neighbor. She
repeatedly renewed five prescriptions once issued to various kids
for medicines, mixing and matching for others as needs arose,
"out of necessity," she said. My heart constricted as I listened
to this local healer describe her efforts to fill in for nonexistent
doctors and nurses.

Moments later, hope returned as I heard Miguel's neighbor
Teresa Caballero say, "If there are four of us here who can be a
voice for the twenty, and the other sixteen can benefit too, we
have to do it." This organizing spirit, I understood, was the community's greatest resource.

In San Elizario, Texas, the Alianza Para El Desarrollo Comu-
nitario (Alliance for Community Development), which would
become one of MCF's first grantees, had been working with *colonia*
residents for four years when we visited, delivering potable water
by truck; assisting with natural gas and sewage service; transforming contracts into manageable deeds; and, at the same time,
providing education and training so residents could advocate and
organize for themselves around daunting everyday issues of chil-

dren's health, environmental protection, and basic services. This savvy interweaving of direct services and community organizing would become a hallmark of MCF's approach in years to come. With the help of Alianza, staffed by *colonia* residents, families were already beginning to test their own power. Residents were knocking on neighbors' doors, encouraging them to register to vote. With pressure from Alianza, the settlements were beginning to appear on county maps, a critical first step toward the goal of establishing legal status and obtaining needed services. "We're knocking harder on their door now," Carlos Jacobo said of local officials. "If it weren't for Alianza, they wouldn't hear us one by one."

If MCF could support this kind of nascent effort, I came to believe, we could ultimately achieve far more than we could through the provision of services alone. *Colonia* residents paid taxes, but they got little to nothing in return. If we could help bring them together and amplify their voices, perhaps they could begin to access not merely charity but the basic services to which they were entitled.

In the meantime, Teresa Caballero, a mother of four, was making do with what she had, just as mothers have done throughout history. She nurtured plants against all odds by feeding them used laundry water and showed other mothers how to chlorinate water to make it safe for drinking. "We're going to have a bath tomorrow!" Teresa's four-year-old daughter Ofelia exclaimed excitedly—the Alianza water truck was scheduled to arrive. Teresa said she blessed the driver each time he pulled away, hurrying to the next *colonia*. Teresa was a natural local leader, one of many I would meet in communities across the country. Alianza helped Teresa and her family, but they also relied on her energy and determination to push for what co-founder Daniel Solis called "basic, dire human needs."

"The poor must talk to the poor because we are the only ones who listen to each other," Teresa insisted. Her words would stay with me over the years to come, informing MCF's efforts to bring people together, build on their connections, and help them raise their voices together. If I did nothing else, I told myself that day in Via Alegre, I would make sure that Teresa and her neighbors were heard.

Chapter 4: From Theory to Practice

There is no such thing as a single-issue struggle because we do not live single-issue lives.

—Audre Lorde

By the time we made our first round of grants in November of 2002, the Marguerite Casey Foundation had established our vision: a more just and equitable society for all, where all children are nurtured to become compassionate, responsible, and self-reliant adults; where families are engaged in the life of their communities, the nation, and the world; and where people take responsibility for meeting today's needs as well as those of future generations. From that vision, we had distilled a mission: to help low-income families strengthen their voices and mobilize their communities in order to achieve that just and equitable society. Finally, we had translated our mission into a concrete funding approach: we would provide sizeable long-term general support grants to organizations that use issue education, advocacy, and activism to advance movement building.

Our faith in our grantees—and our conviction that families are the real experts on what their communities need—is reflected in the nuts and bolts of our grantmaking methodology. For the past eighteen years, the foundation has dedicated virtually our entire grantmaking budget to long-term general support, a prized but hard-to-come-by funding mechanism that puts control in the hands of those doing the work. Nationwide, by comparison, fewer than one-fourth of foundation grants are awarded in the form of general support, and even fewer are multiyear or of significant size. When MCF invests in an organization, we are making a commitment not only of resources but also of faith. We believe in the ability of our grantees to build a movement of low-income families, and we believe that those families know better than anyone what they most need and what they have to offer. This faith underlies our brand promise to "Ask, Listen, Act." It drives our commitment to providing general support, so that *you* decide the best way to empower your community. It also inspires us to provide long-term support, because we understand that social change is a complex process, not a "deliverable" that can be called forth on demand. MCF makes these long-term commitments not to individual leaders but to what we call cornerstone organizations. These are organizations that have deep roots in their communities and play a central and sustained role in the activism of poor communities. They consistently put families at the forefront of their efforts, and they get results.

A trusted founder may retire, key staff may move on, but the relationship between the foundation and these organizations continues, because it is held not by individuals but by working collectives, bound by the common DNA of a shared vision. We do extensive research before we commit to funding a new organization, but once we make that commitment, we don't micromanage. Program officers are there to provide support and counsel, but we don't second guess our grantees by telling them how to spend each dollar.

This level of restraint is unusual in the world of philanthropy. When we started out, it was nearly unheard of. Most philanthropic organizations focused their giving on specific areas—health care, education, etc.—and often generated even narrower short-term initiatives within them. This was not a model we wanted to replicate. Our board and staff understood that movement building requires trust and collaboration, not top-down mandates. We also understood that movement building means taking a long view, which requires long-term funding. If grassroots organizations and the families and communities with whom they work are to succeed, they need a reliable partner to stand with them over time.

Given MCF's modest resources relative to families' needs, we determined early on that we could not support direct services at a level that would have a significant impact. The magnitude of child and family poverty in this country is so great that even if we committed our entire endowment, we could not alleviate it for a single day. In fact, there is *no* amount of charity that can make up for the structural inequities that keep some families in poverty no matter how hard they work, while the rich get richer even as they sleep. What philanthropy can do is help overcome the powerlessness that so often goes hand in hand with poverty. By engaging families in coming up with solutions that they can push for collectively, we believe, MCF can help ensure that being poor does not mean being powerless.

I would argue that long-term general support is the most strategic form of grantmaking, because we get to know the entire organization. We get to talk with grantees about their work on the ground but also about governance, finance, operations, leadership, and how all that is evolving over time. How is the organization growing? Where do they need help? These are important conversations. At the end of the day, if it is done thoughtfully, general support leads to stronger organizations that have greater impact. At the same time, it creates space for innovation, even disruption, because organizations have funds to do what they think is necessary in the moment.

Today, I am pleased to see growing interest within philanthropy in the power and potential of general support. It has been a long and often lonely road to get to this point. When we set out, the bigger, more established foundations that get most of the oxygen in the room did not fund core operating support or advocacy work. Yet here we were, this very young foundation with a new board and president, placing these approaches at the center of our work. We would go to philanthropic meetings, and people would look at us askance: "You're funding advocacy work? You're giving core operating support?" We just kept beating the drum: *this is what is needed.*

An infrastructure of trust

MCF is headquartered in Seattle because that is where Jim Casey and his siblings grew up, but we decided to focus our investments more broadly, targeting resources to regions with the highest concentration of child and family poverty. Using the Annie E. Casey Foundation's *Kids Count Data Book*, we identified four regions in which we would make grants: West, Southwest, South, and Midwest.

In each of these regions, we built relationships with wise and formidable activists whose insights help guide our work to this day. We looked for networks, associations, and civic organizations that were shaping the field while remaining deeply rooted in their communities. We worked to ensure that the organizations we invited to apply for funding were well-respected not only among their peers but also by people who did not necessarily agree with them. We would call elected officials and ask, "Who is pushing you hardest?" Wherever we went, we asked potential grantees the same central question: "What do you need?"

In advance of our first round of funding, we reached out to more than eighty organizations. We used our initial correspondence with these groups to communicate the ways in which MCF's approach was different from what they had likely experienced before. We described our commitment to general operating support and reminded potential applicants that they did not have to reinvent the wheel for us by coming up with a new project or initiative. These were organizations that took their marching orders from the community, and we aimed to keep it that way by supporting work they were *already* doing—a rare offer in the grantmaking world, where funders' desire to make their mark too often forces grantees to take on multiple, competing mandates in order to receive the support they need.

In the early years, it took a lot of communication to help grantees understand that we truly were committed to doing things differently. I would read proposals and notice that groups that were clearly doing advocacy work were afraid of putting the word "advocacy" on paper. I urged them to call it what it was. I wanted them to understand that we were a different kind of foundation. We *wanted* them to be honest. We counted on them to be bold. Still, there was hesitation at the beginning. Years of conditioning had taught them that if they wanted to stay afloat, they had to frame their work in a certain way. We had to undo that conditioning, which meant building trust.

Over time, our grantees came to understand that we existed to support their work, not the reverse. They didn't have to twist themselves into pretzels to keep up with ever-shifting program areas in order to receive funding from MCF. At the same time, we aimed through our grantmaking to act as an agent of change, empowering organizations to do things they might not have thought possible. This was and is a delicate balance, one we are still working to perfect.

From the beginning, the groups that we have chosen to invest in have engaged community members as activists in their own right, not merely figureheads for an organization's agenda. These cornerstone organizations show strength in the face of unbridled power and humility in their interactions with their neighbors. They train youth and parents from low-income neighborhoods and communities of color as leaders, advocates, and organizers. They seek strategic alliances and work to build lasting coalitions. They share a commitment to anti-racist principles, policies, and practices. Finally, they have a track record of success in achieving policy change.

In the beginning, several organizations told us our grantmaking approach was "a breath of fresh air." Others were dubious that we would remain committed to general support and a true spirit of partnership, predicting that, as we consolidated our efforts, we would want to "flex our muscle" by creating issue-driven portfolios. The only way we could overcome this skepticism was to stay the course. Over time, that is exactly what we've done.

Rethinking governance

The Florida sun rippled the asphalt as we began our tour through Little Haiti, 3.5 square miles comprising the oldest neighborhood of people of Haitian descent in Florida and one of the largest communities of Haitians in the United States. Riding in a long yellow school bus, MCF board members listened to Boukman Mangones, a Haitian American architect, speak about the fight to stop real estate developers from displacing the community and to preserve Little Haiti's heritage. Mangones was joined by Marleine Bastien, the founder and executive director of Fanm Ayisyen Nan Miyami (FANM), a relatively new grantee. Glad to be meeting the board for the first time in her home community, Bastien graciously opened up her organization to us, eager to ensure that funders know the struggles low-income Haitian families experience every day. When the bus tour ended, board members spent the afternoon in FANM's office, joined by four other grantees who were grappling with various issues troubling the community, from gentrification to climate change.

During my first two decades in philanthropy, I sat through far too many meetings where poverty was discussed in the abstract and those in charge of much-needed resources made decisions on behalf of people they had never met. I also experienced this firsthand during my family's early years in the United States, when we were struggling to get our footing and dealing with the reality of poverty ourselves. These experiences convinced me that if we were going to address poverty, poor people needed to be not just in the room but taking the lead, telling us what they needed rather than the other way around. We have designed every aspect of our work—including our unusual approach to governance—with this principle in mind. We do everything we can to avoid an all-too-familiar scenario: a room full of "experts" pontificating about poverty over a catered meal, while those who have experienced poverty firsthand are nowhere to be found.

In particular, we have structured the board's role and activities in a way that minimizes the traditional distance and brings board members into direct relationship with those doing the work on the ground. Instead of demanding that grantees come to them—or shutting out grantee voices altogether—the board of directors holds its quarterly meetings in grantee communities. By traveling to the communities we serve and speaking directly with the people who live there, our board members are able to understand poverty in its complex, multidimensional reality rather than through the filter of a report or statistics. Over the past five years alone, eighty-eight different grantees have spoken directly with the board. These on-the-ground encounters remove "living in poverty" from the sterility of statistics and create the space for mutual accountability.

"It is not often that we get to meet with the board of our funders, and it was very powerful to speak to them all," Bastien said of her experience. "They were able to see firsthand the million things that are important for low- to moderate-income families but that cannot fit in a grant and most importantly, they heard it directly from the members themselves."

What I love about our board is that they do not begin conversations with grantees by offering advice. Instead, they ask questions like: "What do you need in order to change your conditions? What can we do to help?" (and always, Board Chair Freeman Hrabowski's trademark query, "What gives you hope?").

I often say that MCF's board of directors is our greatest asset.

After so many years in traditional philanthropy, I had grown accustomed to dancing around my more radical goals, couching them in language I thought would be acceptable. I used to joke that I was a walking thesaurus for organizing and social change because I had so many ways to talk about these things without actually using those terms.

Things are different with the MCF board. I don't need to mince words when I'm talking with them because they truly own the foundation's values. They aren't shy about telling me when they think I've veered off track, but no one is asking me to avoid controversy. Our board members are genuine partners, invested in this endeavor at the deepest level. By asking hard questions, allowing space for big-picture conversation and taking chances on new ideas, the MCF board has kept the foundation on the cutting edge for nearly twenty years.

The risks the foundation has taken would not have been possible with a large, remote board of directors that met infrequently and relied on committees. Instead, our dedicated board has enabled the foundation to maintain our focus even in the face of opposition or controversy.

"Is the foundation's direction risky?" asked Dr. Bill Foege, a founding board member who has since retired. "Only in the sense that solid prevention efforts take time and this might not satisfy those wanting to see results this year. We know enough about history to know that if strong institutions are in place to help families, and if they find their voices, they will rise to their own destiny, break the chains of poverty, and help every generation that follows."

Whatever we have been able to achieve over the years is a testament to the contributions of the founding board members

who have stayed with us for the long haul: Freeman Hrabowski, Douglas Patiño, Pat Schroeder, and Bill Foege. They could
so easily have put the brakes on the shift toward movement
building—that would have been the safer choice politically—but
instead they embraced it. Along with the rest of the MCF board,
they have shepherded the foundation with generosity and grace.

As Board Chair Freeman Hrabowski puts it, "The strength of
the board is in its members' different experiences." I would add
that while each brings a different life experience to the work, they
all share a bone-deep commitment to the battle against poverty
and racial injustice. I love standing back and watching each of
them interact with grantees and families.

As a child, Freeman participated in Martin Luther King's his-
toric Children's Crusade in Birmingham, Alabama, in 1963. He
remembers dogs chasing him and people spitting on him. At
twelve years old, he spent five nights in jail. He knows hatred
and injustice in his bones, but he also knows what it means to lay
your life on the line in the name of change.

The president of the University of Maryland, Baltimore County, Freeman is a teacher to the core. I saw this side of him as
early as 2002, when the board embarked on its first site visit with
grantees. Freeman immediately gravitated toward a young child.
Soon they were working through a math problem together. By
the end of the visit, they had an answer, and this child had a new
sense of his own abilities. Freeman does this kind of thing constantly. Wherever he travels, people are surprised to encounter
a prominent educator who is not telling kids, "Here's what you
need to do," but instead is asking them questions like "What's
your favorite subject?" and "How can I help you?"

Pat Schroeder, another longtime board member, faced more

than her share of discrimination as the first woman from Colorado elected to the United States House of Representatives and the first woman to serve on the House Armed Services Committee. Pat is famous, among other things, for answering a query about how she could be a member of Congress while raising two children by saying, "I have a brain and a uterus and they both work." Like Freeman, Pat instantly took to the idea of "Ask, Listen, Act" and has helped us build a board culture premised on a commitment to listening to poor families.

Bill Foege is a giant in his field of global health and epidemiology. He is the former director of the Centers for Disease Control and Prevention and is credited with devising the global strategy that led to the eradication of smallpox in the 1970s. He has spent his career championing child health and development in poor communities. I always remember Bill saying that in our mission to end poverty, we had to see the last mile and then work to get there.

Douglas Patiño has four decades of service in academia, politics, and philanthropy. He was a cabinet member focused on employment and economic security under former Arizona governor Bruce Babbitt and former California governor Jerry Brown and is vice chancellor emeritus for the California State University system. He is one of the chief architects of MCF's grantmaking model and has dedicated his life to social justice.

Each of our board members has brought something unique to the table. I remember many hours spent talking with Ruth Massinga, a founding board member who came to us from Casey Family Programs, where she was president and CEO. Our early conversations were exhilarating as we ranged through possibilities I had long dreamed of pursuing but had not been fully able to explore within the constraints of traditional philanthropy. MCF owes its philosophical freedom to Ruth. She became the protector of what we were trying to create. When people tried to push the foundation in another direction, she told them, "MCF has its own mission. Let it evolve."

Grantmaking beyond silos

I sometimes say that I understand the Pacific Northwest because I know how it feels for the salmon to swim upstream. One aspect of this challenge became clear to me at one of the first convenings for our new grantees. We were just getting started when a community leader approached me to complain about the seating arrangements. "Why I am sitting with people who do education?" she queried. "I am a housing expert!"

"That's wonderful," I told her politely. "Perhaps you can contribute your expertise to a conversation about how place influences the quality of a child's education."

Her words have stayed with me over the years because, however unintentionally, she articulated one of the greatest challenges to the foundation's ongoing effort to spark and support a cross-issue movement: the inclination to hunker down in silos rather than tackling the web of interconnected issues in which so many poor families are entangled.

This woman was not an outlier. She was simply being carried along by a powerful current within philanthropy itself. At some point every foundation, no matter the size, comes up against the limits of its endowment. For funders that have taken on poverty as a central challenge, these limits can be particularly stark. The scale of poverty in the United States is so vast that it dwarfs even the most generous endowment. Many philanthropies deal with this challenge by narrowing the scope of their efforts. By focusing on a particular issue, they are able to carve out an arena in which they believe they can be successful. There is certainly practical value in this approach, and issue-driven funders have made significant progress on a number of fronts. But the more time we spent listening to families, the clearer it became that they do not experience poverty as a set of discrete issues. Instead, the daily challenges that come with being poor are so deeply intertwined as to be inseparable. Economic stability depends on consistent employment, which requires quality child care, reliable transportation, and an education that instills the skills necessary to compete in an information economy. Residential segregation is connected to educational inequity, which is in turn related to racialized over-policing. Immigration policy is intertwined with public health, which directly influences child well-being. Tackling one challenge at a time may be satisfying in the near term, but in the long run, it leaves families without the cohesive supports they need.

As MCF developed our grantmaking framework, we were resolute in our commitment to a boundary-crossing approach. We understood that cultivating a cross-issue movement would be a challenge in a silo-dotted landscape where "turf" was the very ground beneath our feet. But our mandate from families was clear. Again and again, they told us that their experience of poverty bore little resemblance to the strategies most often used to ameliorate it.

We began our journey by looking for organizations that shared our broader vision. One of the first site visits we made was to the Community Coalition in Los Angeles. They told us how a thriving middle-class African American neighborhood had been blindsided by the crack epidemic. Instead of enjoying a hard-earned retirement, grandparents were taking care of children whose parents had become addicted. When they sought help, these hard-working grandparents wound up spending hours on the bus tracking down scattered services. Community Coalition addressed this by bringing services to families in their own community. MCF supported this approach with great enthusiasm. In fact, Community Coalition remains a grantee to this day. They understand their constituency in a deep and lasting way.

From time to time, I still think of the woman at that early convening who objected to being seated with those outside her field. The attitude her discomfort reflected is far from obsolete today, but I do believe the conversation has shifted since then. Activists on the leading edge of change are increasingly adopting a multi-issue focus and actively seeking ways to work together. As I speak and work with grantee leaders and constituents across the country, this is the perspective I hear expressed. More and more, our grantees share with us a core understanding that the challenges they and their constituents face are profoundly interconnected and must be tackled collectively if real change is the goal. That is what collective impact is about.

No unsolicited proposals

Among the most controversial elements of MCF's grantmaking process is our decision not to accept unsolicited proposals. This approach makes sense to us for several reasons. One is our desire to run a lean organization where funds are directed to grantees rather than overhead. A smaller team leaves more funds for grantmaking, our *raison d'etre*. Reading through unsolicited proposals is extremely labor-intensive, pulling staff time and energy away from the long-term relationship building that is key to our practice. By accepting only invited proposals, we are able to focus our energy on delving deeply into the communities in which we fund. Coupled with clear grantmaking priorities, this allows us to identify and build relationships with organizations that truly meet the needs of those communities.

The approach we have taken certainly brings its own challenges—primarily, being sure we are finding the right organizations to advance the work. We addressed this by establishing clear criteria for the groups we would fund: cornerstone organizations that were committed to organizing and leadership development among low-income families, with the long-term aim of changing public policy.

Knowing what we were looking for was one thing. Finding it was another. Fortunately, the research process that launched our first round of grantmaking also helped us establish a network of sources in communities across the country—individuals who had an ear to the ground and could steer us toward groups doing strong work in their communities. To this day, we rely on our network of grantees to introduce us to others whose work they admire. Because this entails trusting communities and their leaders to help us, it takes some of the mystery out of the grantmaking process and deepens the sense of partnership between the foundation and our grantees.

The moment of truth

In the fall of 2002, MCF announced our first round of grantees. Identifying them had been an exhilarating process, introducing us to an army of activists around the country. Through these initial grants—many of which have been renewed several times, some up to this day—we began to understand the tremendous, untapped potential of families and communities in our nation's poorest regions. When you plug a parent's fervent commitment to her children's well-being into the infrastructure of a nonprofit organization with deep roots in the community, you create a powerful alliance. By supporting these organizations over the long haul and helping them grow, you begin to build the infrastructure for a movement.

We looked hard for groups that placed leadership development among low-income families at the heart of their campaigns, regardless of issue. In the process, we discovered groups like Asian Immigrant Women Advocates in Oakland, California, which was developing an intergenerational leadership training program for garment workers and their families. A grant to the Washington, D.C.–based College Summit supported efforts to help low-income students reach college by training parents and teachers to guide them. In Montgomery, Alabama, a grant to the Federation of Child Care Centers of Alabama, Inc. allowed them to develop and disseminate a model program for increasing parent and community involvement in child care issues.

From our very first grantmaking round, we sought opportunities to bring people together. In Illinois, we were honored to support a coalition of African, Asian, European, and Latino immigrants working together to enhance grassroots leadership among low-income families in Chicago's diverse immigrant communities. A grant to the National Interfaith Committee for Worker Justice bolstered their capacity to organize and strengthen interfaith worker justice groups in the South, the Southwest, Chicago, and California.

Our commitment to supporting anti-racism efforts was reflected in grants to groups like the New Orleans–based People's Institute for Survival and Beyond, which was developing anti-racism training and curricula along with a national youth agenda. In Charleston, West Virginia, we supported the Commission on Religion in Appalachia, Inc. in their effort to develop a critical mass of Appalachian parent leaders who affirmed a shared anti-racism analysis.

With this first round of grants, we established what would be an ongoing commitment to leadership development among low-income youth. Grants to groups like Chicago's Chinese Mutual Aid Association and the Seattle Young People's Project supported youth-led organizing around a range of issues at the local, state, and national levels.

Over the course of our first eighteen months, we made more than 30 million dollars in grants to promote organizing, advocacy and activism by working families. Grants to groups like the Los Angeles Alliance for a New Economy (LAANE), the Metropolitan Tenants Organization in Chicago, Parent Voices in San Francisco, and Southern Echo in Jackson, Mississippi, inaugurated relationships that would evolve into long-term partnerships. We made grants to organizations that supported family leaders in their efforts to combat abuses in the juvenile justice system; challenged elected officials to recognize the needs of low-income constituents; and advocated for a living wage.

We funded nascent multiracial coalitions working to advance the democratic participation of low-income families. As anti-Muslim and anti-immigrant sentiment flared in the wake of 9/11, we focused resources on efforts to protect families from hate crimes and other forms of discrimination. We launched what would be a long-term relationship with the *colonias* along the U.S.-Mexico border and with Native American communities from Arizona to Washington State.

We learned a tremendous amount from that first round of grantees. At the same time, we were laying the groundwork for the next phase of our work: bringing these remarkable organizations together in the hope of sparking a national family-led movement that would challenge the notion that poverty is an inevitable aspect of American life. It was a lofty goal, but one that our encounters with these remarkable individuals and organizations left us more inspired than ever to hope for and pursue.

Chapter 5: The Story of Poverty

Philanthropy is commendable, but it must not cause the philanthropist to overlook the circumstances of economic injustice which make philanthropy necessary.

—*Rev. Martin Luther King Jr.*

I was thirteen years old when my family was plunged into poverty, seemingly overnight. One moment, we were living in a big house in Nicaragua, where my father was a prominent lawyer. We had everything we needed and more. Then, in a moment, the political climate changed and we found ourselves exiled, starting over again in America. In a matter of weeks, we lost everything we had, except for the most important thing: one another.

The experience of going from material comfort to stark poverty as a result of political shifts beyond our control left me deeply convinced that poverty is not a personal characteristic, much less a personal failing. It is simply a situation—one in which any of us can find ourselves at any moment. The truth is, families move in and out of poverty.

What people tend to miss when they talk about poverty is the power of reciprocity—the way poor families survive by looking out for one another. When I speak of the abiding strength of family, I am not talking about the concept of "resilience." I loathe that word, especially when it is used to romanticize the lives of children in poverty. Talk of resilience in this context is just another version of the self-exonerating "bootstraps" mentality. When we call a child "resilient," what we're really doing is abdicating our own responsibility to her by telling ourselves she is tough enough to make it on her own no matter how many obstacles are thrown in her path.

Reciprocity is something altogether different. When you value reciprocity, you are honoring the bonds among family members. You don't use a family's own strength as an excuse to abandon it; you look for ways to fortify family connections and support collective effort so that family can make the most of the resources available to it. Reciprocity is what allowed my own family to make it. Our commitment to one another allowed us to survive and eventually to flourish.

When I was in my sophomore year of college, I switched to night classes so I could work full time during the day to help support my family. I never questioned that this was the right thing to do, or saw it as some great sacrifice, because nothing was ever a one-way street in my family. I supported my family, they supported me, and that was how all of us managed to get by.

I was able to take those night classes even though I couldn't afford a car because my father took three buses several nights a week to meet me at school and ride those same three buses back home with me. Sometimes my sister or brother would come instead. It was a long trip for them—if we missed the McAllister bus, we'd get home at midnight. But I learned an essential lesson from this experience: families have their own solutions. They know how to help one another succeed. This does not mean the larger society should leave poor families to fend for themselves, but it does mean that no one—including philanthropists—should assume they know better than those families what they need or how they should live.

Since our inception, the Marguerite Casey Foundation has adhered to the philosophy that the health and well-being of children are inextricably linked to those of their families. Children are not separate little adults. They're not poor because they didn't go out and get a job. They're poor because their families are poor. Yet the field still falls back on terms like "child poverty" that bear little relation to the reality of families' lives. I don't know where this tendency stems from. It may be that it's easier to gain public sympathy, and public funding, by talking about "innocent children" rather than dealing with the complexities of families. But we do more harm than good when we create funding models, whether public or private, that operate as if children and parents don't eat from the same pot. This false dichotomy contributes to the culture of family separation—if you want to help poor kids you have to "rescue" them from their families—when the reality is that if we truly cared about kids, we would work to address the needs of the whole family.

At MCF, we see fighting poverty and empowering families as two sides of the same coin. Funders may do harm when, even with the best intentions, we limit our anti-poverty efforts to the provision of services. Concrete supports are essential, but it is also crucial to remember that poor people are more than merely vessels of need. At MCF, we see families living in poverty as a resource, not just a collection of deficits and demands. We understand that poor people have pressing needs, but also that they hold tremendous potential. Tapping into this potential requires much more than charity. It's going to take a movement.

Contempt for the poor

More than 42 million people in the United States are living in poverty on any given day, according to federal figures. High as this number is, we believe it is actually a vast undercount, reflecting only those Americans who live below the outdated federal poverty threshold of about 12,000 dollars a year, or 25,000 dollars for a family of four. Many more—100 million, or a third of all Americans—are economically insecure, defined as living below 200 percent of the federal poverty rate. Forty-three percent of American households don't bring in enough money to cover basics like food, housing, child care, transportation, and a cell phone. However you measure it, here in the richest country in the world, poverty remains appallingly widespread.

Work is no remedy for this kind of pervasive poverty. As it stands, the majority of poor families are headed by working adults who spend long hours at low-wage jobs that offer few to no benefits. According to a recent report from the Irvine Foundation, half of all workers in California make wages that keep them at the poverty level. This is where we believe the crucial injustice resides: in the unconscionable gap between what it costs to live and what it pays to work.

The past decade has seen the longest economic expansion on record in this country, but the workers on whose labor that expansion depends have not shared in the fruits of a growing economy. The federal minimum wage has remained stuck at $7.25 an hour for more than a decade—the longest run in history without a cost-of-living adjustment. Meanwhile, researchers at the Massachusetts Institute of Technology have determined that a *living* wage—one which meets the basic needs of a family of four—would be $16.14 an hour, well over twice the current legal minimum. That means we expect minimum-wage workers to find a way to provide for a family on less than half of the bare minimum they need. When they struggle—missing a rent payment in order to keep the lights on; skimping on food at the end of the month; making do with substandard child care or none at all—rather than supporting them, we bury them in an avalanche of blame. In the worst-case scenario, we call poverty neglect and take away their children. This helps explain why, at the very beginning, MCF decided we had to do much more than improve conditions for kids in foster care. If we wanted to support families, that meant attacking poverty, and the blame we heap upon those who are living with it, straight on.

In 2017, Philip Alston, the United Nations special rapporteur on extreme poverty and human rights, came to the United States to investigate the causes and effects of systemic poverty in this wealthiest of nations. What struck me most about his report were his piercing observations about the American attitude toward the poor. The America Alston described is a land of "private wealth and public squalor" where contempt for the poor has made criminalization and stigma our frontline response to those in need. "Punishing and imprisoning the poor," he wrote, "is the distinctively American response to poverty in the twenty-first century."

This response is inextricable from the American legacy of racism and racial exploitation. The United States, Alston wrote, "remains a chronically segregated society" where blacks are 2.5 times more likely than whites to be living in poverty. "The structural racism that keeps a large percentage of non-whites in poverty and near poverty," he noted with a directness rarely found in American discourse, can only be explained "by long-standing structural discrimination on the basis of race, reflecting the enduring legacy of slavery."

"Locking up the poor precisely because they are poor, greatly exaggerating the amount of fraud in the system, shaming those who need assistance, and devising ever more obstacles to prevent people from getting needed benefits, is not a strategy to reduce or eliminate poverty," he wrote in a withering summary. "It seems driven primarily by contempt, and sometimes even by hatred for the poor, along with a 'winner takes all' mentality."

The notion of poverty as a personal failing is far from a new one. In 1776, economist Adam Smith defined poverty as the inability to afford "not only the commodities which are indispensably necessary for the support of life, but whatever the custom of the country renders it indecent for creditable people, even of the lowest order, to be without."

We haven't progressed much in our attitudes in the two-hundred-plus years since. To this day, the Merriam-Webster dictionary defines poverty as "the state of one who lacks a usual or socially acceptable amount of money or material possessions." Poverty is seen as a lack not merely of money but of human worth—an individual failure rather than a structural problem. This is poverty as defined from the outside, looking in. Poverty as an *experience*—the father who holds down two $7.25-an-hour jobs and rarely sees the family he works so hard to feed; the mother who picks raspberries in the baking sun, yet does not earn enough money to buy fresh produce for her own children—is glaringly absent from the public discourse. As the nineteenth-century novelist Herman Melville aptly put it, "Of all the preposterous assumptions of humanity, nothing exceeds the criticisms made of the habits of the poor by the well-housed, well-warmed, and well-fed." Yet these criticisms ring far louder than the voices of experience.

Words hold tremendous power to shape public perception, and perception, in turn, shapes policy. Until we challenge the negative, blame-laden language used to describe poverty—from the op-ed page to the campaign trail to the dictionary itself—policymakers will have a license to dismantle programs that provide an economic toehold for poor families and to abdicate any responsibility to create policies that help lift people out of poverty.

Redefining poverty away from blame and toward solutions demands that we shift our conception of poverty from something that happens to "others"—an ill-defined, depersonalized mass whom we either blame for their situation or else ignore entirely—toward a more inclusive and realistic vision. It means recognizing that poverty is a situation rather than a character flaw—a situation to which few Americans are immune. A medical crisis, a layoff, the birth of a child who has special needs, the collapse of an industry, or even a bad mortgage can be all it takes to push a family over the brink into poverty. Yet America so prides itself on being a country without poverty—land of equality, home to the great middle class—that "poor" has become the nation's most taboo four-letter word.

Individuals who dare to describe the challenges they face raising families in poverty are blamed for their own struggles: they are lazy, undeserving, morally as well as financially lacking. Those who speak of poverty as a social problem are accused of inciting "class warfare." In the political arena, terms such as "low-income," "income inequality," "low-wage workers," and even "working class" are used to gloss over the painful reality of a hungry child or an eviction notice.

The flip side of blame is invisibility. As Jeff Shesol noted in *The New Yorker*, "in the half century since [President Lyndon] Johnson pledged 'not only to relieve the symptom of poverty, but to cure it and, above all, to prevent it,' presidents of both parties have shown a rare, bipartisan resolve to avoid the subject." In a search of fifty State of the Union and similar key speeches, Shesol found "very few mentions of 'poverty' or the 'poor' after Johnson left office." In my own work, I see people literally talk past poor people who are in the room as if they don't exist or have an opinion worth hearing.

Invisibility provides perfect cover for inaction. In the decades that followed Johnson's famous declaration of a "war on poverty," journalist Sasha Abramsky has observed, "We have witnessed a great unraveling of large parts of the social safety net and an extraordinary willingness to believe the worst about the poor. Linguistically, from 1964 to today, the dominant discourse has shifted from seeing poverty as the problem to framing poor people and their perceived dysfunctions as the primary challenge. It makes it far harder today to push for the kind of big-picture anti-poverty strategy that was born in 1964."

Holly Baker, an MCF grantee from the Farmworker Association of Florida, astutely described what this culture of blame and invisibility means for poor families themselves: "Poverty is not only struggling to have the means to support the basic needs of your family; poverty is living each day feeling and knowing that you are unjustly judged by others and that you don't have an equal voice."

From self-blame to shared struggle

Early on in my career in philanthropy, I attended a conference where we were asked to participate in a simulation of poverty. I was handed a baby doll and told to play the part of a single mom with three children. My assignment was to keep them fed, clothed, and educated on a minimum-wage income while navigating the various systems and institutions with which poor people are required to interact.

Needless to say, things quickly fell apart. I had to leave work early to drop off a rent check, much to my boss's displeasure, then race to the six-year-old's school for a parent/teacher conference. Flustered, I put the "baby" on a chair while I dug in my purse for his older sister's report card. The next thing I knew, the school had placed a call to social services, triggering a neglect investigation.

By the time I got out of there, I'd missed my bus, and the little ones were getting fretful, so I took them straight home instead of stopping to buy food for the weekend. When we finally made it back to our tiny apartment, there was an eviction notice taped to the door. I called the property manager to remind him I'd paid the rent, but he demanded a receipt, which I had not been given. The moment I put the phone down, it was ringing again—Social Services was calling to schedule a home visit to determine whether I was fit to parent my own children. One bad day and everything I had was on the line: my home, my job, my family itself.

I got the message: I was doing a terrible job of being a poor person. But rather than scrambling to catch up with an impossible barrage of competing demands, I decided to shift the focus of the scenario. I didn't want to prove that I could do a better job of being poor. I wanted to challenge the structural barriers that make it impossible for all families living in poverty to meet the competing demands placed upon them. At the same time, I wanted to demonstrate what can happen when a community works together.

The first thing I did was go speak to my neighbor. She had been there when I paid my rent and, when I asked, agreed to testify on my behalf. The eviction was stayed, and my family had a roof over our heads for another night. Just as importantly, I had succeeded in shifting the narrative from one that focused on the individual failures of those who are struggling with poverty to one that focused on our collective power.

Looking back, I see the seeds of MCF's *modus operandi* in that little scenario. We invest in the poorest regions of the country, but we also seek areas where we see clear potential for collaborative action. We're not in this to save a soul or two. Our aim is to galvanize entire communities to support lasting change. At the same time, we are constantly working to change the narrative about poverty from one of personal failure (she put the baby down!) to one of structural failure (why didn't she have access to safe, affordable child care?).

In everything we do, MCF is working toward two interconnected goals: to eradicate poverty and the suffering it brings and, as a prerequisite, to transform the narrative about what it means to be poor. We aspire to a world where every family has what it needs in order to thrive, resources are distributed equitably, and poverty no longer exists. To get there, we must counter once and for all the toxic lie that allows us to tolerate ever-widening inequality and to countenance suffering in the face of plenty. I'm talking about the notion that poverty is a personal rather than a systemic failure—that poor people themselves, rather than the economic systems that exploit their labor to enrich others, are the root cause of poverty. From this corrupt and corrosive narrative flows much unnecessary suffering, as well as tremendous undeserved wealth.

Two wings of the same bird

MCF aims to tackle both faces of poverty: the material hardship and the moral censure. Through our grantmaking, network-weaving, and other movement building efforts, we strive to improve the daily lives of low-income families. At the same time, through our communications arm, we are engaged in a parallel effort to change the story this country tells itself about poverty, and poor families in particular.

Poverty means you don't have material resources adequate to your needs. But it also means you're deprived of your voice. When you say something, it is devalued because you are poor. In order to build a strong base of families working to change polices for their own betterment, we realized, MCF had to tackle the pernicious invisibility of poverty in America and find a way for families to be heard.

This is why we see grantmaking and communications as two wings of the same bird. Communications at MCF doesn't mean sitting around pontificating about poverty from the comfort of our desks. Instead, we work to shift the balance of power so that poor families have an opportunity to speak for themselves. Through our communications efforts, we aim to elevate the voices of poor and working families and underscore *their* solutions to the problems they face. Rather than using our communications arm to promote the work of the foundation and enhance our own reputation, we deploy that capacity strategically to advance our larger goal of movement building.

Like so much of our work, our commitment to shifting the narrative about poverty dates back to the Listening Circles we conducted early on. Public perception, participants observed, has a profound impact on public policy, for better or—more often—for worse. Want to cut welfare? Plant pernicious stories about high-living "welfare queens." Need funding to build more prisons? Promote the myth of the teenage "super-predator." For too long, conservatives had hijacked the national agenda by controlling the narrative, while community organizations lacked the infrastructure to push back. Listening Circle participants recognized this dynamic and asked us to help challenge it by creating forums for families living in poverty to tell their own stories.

Over the years, this effort has taken many forms. In 2000, we hosted a convening designed to help grantees use social media to mobilize constituents, advance policy, raise money, and tell their stories. In 2005, we published our first white paper, "Different Incomes, Common Dreams," a comprehensive look at public attitudes about poverty in America before and after Hurricane Katrina.

Because traditional media tend to feature a limited range of recognized "expert" voices, we found that it took constant effort to promote families as the experts on their own lives and get the media to pay attention. In the long run, we determined, if low-income families were to have a consistent voice, they would need their own outlet. In late 2009, we launched *Equal Voice News* (*EVN*), an online newspaper designed to shift the national conversation around poverty by highlighting family voices and concerns. *EVN* seeks to advance the work of our grantees and their constituents through well-reported news stories on issues that have particular resonance for poor and working families—subjects that are often ignored or downplayed by other media outlets. In addition to producing original reporting, *EVN* provides a vehicle for activists, organizers, and thought leaders who are concerned about poverty, inequality, and racial justice to broadcast their perspectives to a wide audience.

Staffed by seasoned reporters and editors, *EVN* has won more than forty journalism awards and continues to produce multimedia content that elevates family voices alongside grantee perspectives. Through our Equal Voice Journalism Fellowship and Scholarship awards, which support professional journalists and journalism students interested in covering poverty and inequality, we also work to diversify the field while increasing public understanding of poverty.

Through *EVN* and other communications efforts, MCF's grantees and their constituents are flinging open the closet door on poverty and defining their lives on their own terms. They are trying, as our board chair, Freeman Hrabowski, has put it, to "encourage robust dialogue that is sometimes uncomfortable, but necessary." As they speak out, they challenge the culture of blame and shame that surrounds poverty in America, painting a picture of courage in the face of disadvantage.

Told from the inside out, the story of poverty is not a tale of personal or moral failing. It is an account of a structural problem with devastating personal implications—a story of racism, injustice, and unfettered greed that traps entire generations despite heroic personal effort. Poverty in *this* story is living in a neighborhood that has liquor stores and payday loan shops but no grocery stores or banks. Poverty is having to choose between paying the rent and putting food on the table. Poverty means living with constant anxiety. It means lighting candles when the electricity goes out, then staying awake all night for fear of burning down the apartment. It means struggling to comfort a sick child while holding out as long as possible before taking her to the doctor, because doing so will mean another unpayable bill. It means trying to convince your kids that cereal for dinner is a treat or, worse, watching those children go hungry even as we throw away tons of food each day. This, to me, is the most unconscionable aspect of poverty in this country—that it exists in the midst of such extraordinary wealth.

Poverty is a thief that keeps getting away with the same crime again and again: the theft of hope from one generation to the next. Poverty robs people of opportunities to live a good life. It robs parents of opportunities to help their children grow and be successful. It robs families of their health. It robs individuals of the opportunity to get an education and pursue a career.

When we do talk about poverty in this country, we act as if it were a single, discrete ailment, like it's "I have a toothache and I'm going to get it fixed." But poverty is not a single tooth that can be extracted while leaving those around it intact. Families experience poverty as an ensnaring web of interrelated issues that radiate from a center of financial insecurity. Yes, poverty is about money, but it is also about education, child care, health care, housing, community safety, transportation, jobs, and justice, or the lack thereof.

Poverty is not an abstraction at MCF because poor *people* are not an abstraction to us. They are partners in our work and part of our daily lives—valued advisors and allies in this journey. The same is true when it comes to racism and race. We are an organization where the majority of the staff and board, as well as our grantees and their constituents, are people of color. We do not have the luxury of treating racism as an abstraction, or one "issue area" among others. Like it or not, it is woven into the fabric of our daily lives and work.

A new narrative

If we truly intend to change the economic trajectory in this country, we need to change the story we tell ourselves about poverty and wealth. And if we want a new narrative, we need a new narrator.

For too long, the national discourse on poverty has been dominated by those with strong opinions but little or no personal experience. Poor people themselves confront a subtle but all-pervasive silencing. Even when their own lives are the topic at hand, their voices are glaringly absent. That is why MCF consistently works to elevate the voices and perspectives of those with the deepest expertise—the families who have experienced poverty firsthand—until they are heard in the rooms where decisions are made about their lives.

Over the years, I've spent countless hours on the road, visiting our grantmaking regions and listening to constituents. In Chicago, I met a homeless man who worked two jobs but was unable to save enough for a security deposit on an apartment. In Kentucky, I visited a man who lived with his daughter in a trailer in front of a mountain that threatened to collapse at any moment, taking their home down with it. In Mississippi, I met a grandmother who had learned to read at age forty. She worked alongside three daughters and a granddaughter at a fish processing plant until it relocated to Mexico, leaving the whole family destitute. In post–Katrina New Orleans, I met a young mother who was working two minimum-wage jobs to pay for the propane tank that heated her family's emergency trailer. Each of these encounters underscored the central lesson I learned from my own experience growing up: the greatest resource any family has in the face of poverty is one another. Yet, paradoxically, of all the pressures that can break down the family structure, the most prevalent, and insidious, is poverty itself.

In 2010, the United Nations replaced the outdated Human Poverty Index with the more nuanced Multidimensional Poverty Index, which looks at indicators including nutrition, education, access to clean water, and, of course, assets. What even this index cannot capture, however, is the *experience* of poverty—an experience that varies not only from one demographic to another but from one family to the next. As part of our ongoing effort to take our mandate from those most affected, we have challenged ourselves to consider more deeply the question, "How do you define poverty?" It is a question we ask both ourselves and our constituents, and we are continually impressed by the range and depth of answers we receive.

I met Charles Jenkins through the Chicago Coalition for the Homeless. A soft-spoken black man who keeps his greying hair tucked beneath a Chicago Cubs cap, Jenkins offered this trenchant response: "Poverty is when you work a full-time job and you don't have enough to put food on your table. Any time you work forty hours a week, and you cannot bring home an honest paycheck that you can in turn live off, that's poverty."

"The ruling class grabs up all of the resources and keeps them just for themselves and only divvies up enough to wet the beaks of those of us that live at or below poverty level," Jenkins continued. "In a country as rich as this one, we should invest in the least among us."

Ernest Johnson, a longtime warrior in the battle for a fairer justice system, views poverty through the lens of opportunity. "My definition of poverty is an oppressive system that doesn't allow families equal opportunities in finance, in education, in the juvenile justice reform discussion, in housing," he said. "Anything that oppresses people and doesn't give them the equal opportunity to have balance so that they can be productive in their lives."

In 2016, MCF held a series of roundtables in three of our grantmaking areas that are home to especially high concentrations of low-wage workers: Jackson, Mississippi; Baton Rouge, Louisiana; and Los Angeles, California. The families we spoke with in these cities echoed Jenkins' analysis. "Wages here have not kept up with the cost of living," said a working mother in Los Angeles, where housing prices have skyrocketed in the past decade. "We're not getting what we need to survive, even though we work all the time. We need a higher minimum wage so we can survive in Los Angeles, but we also need a higher minimum wage so we can raise our own dignity."

The jobs held by the working poor are some of the toughest in the country: cleaning houses and hotel rooms, picking up garbage, scrubbing dishes and pots, diapering children. Although the current unemployment rate is low by historical standards, those who are employed have less job security than in the past because the economy has shifted from one in which most workers expected to spend their entire careers with the same employer (or at least in the same industry) to one in which layoffs are more frequent and wholesale career changes more likely. As a result, hundreds of thousands of low-wage working families struggle to survive from one paycheck to the next. Planning for a secure future is close to impossible.

When I see people living in extreme poverty, as I do whenever I visit our grantees around the country, I don't feel pity. I feel shame. To see such poverty existing in the midst of tremendous excess makes you wonder what we have become. We live in a moment when the net worth of the wealthiest 1 percent of American households exceeds that of the bottom 95 percent. This wealth gap is only accelerating. According to researchers at the University of California, Berkeley, the 400 richest Americans now own more of the country's wealth than the 150 million adults in the bottom 60 percent of wealth distribution.

Meanwhile, working families are up against a reality I remember well from my own early years in this country: being poor is expensive. If you're lucky enough to have a grocery store in your neighborhood, you will pay exorbitant prices for low-quality goods cast off by wealthier neighborhoods—withered produce, stale baked goods, frozen chicken white with frost. Entities like the payday lending industry flood low-income communities for the sole purpose of profiting off poverty, charging interest rates as high as 400 percent for loans that get working families from one paycheck to the next but eliminate any possibility of long-term stability. "If you look at how we are being ripped off, in some places it's dollar for dollar," said a mother of four in Indianola, Mississippi. "We work and work and can't make ends meet."

In the midst of the hate-filled rhetoric that swirls around people living in poverty, I am struck by the simplicity of the equation that rules their daily lives: stagnant wages plus rising costs equals thousands of people who work multiple jobs, commute vast distances, sacrifice their families and their health, and still find themselves unable to make ends meet. And still we tell ourselves that the poor are to blame for their own plight.

Making poverty visible

Poverty is America's dirty secret. We don't like to talk about it, and we don't want to see it. This is why we are constantly "redeveloping" inner cities and "cleaning up" homeless encampments, shuffling people from one place to the next so they don't interfere with our sense of ourselves as the land of opportunity.

This poses a conundrum for the foundation: how do we address poverty in a country that prefers to pretend it does not exist? Early on, we struggled simply to find the right vocabulary. Some objected to using the word "poor" out of concern that the word itself was stigmatizing. At one point we brought in a famous linguist who gave us a convoluted two-paragraph definition of poverty to use in lieu of the word itself. Various other alternatives surfaced—"low-wealth," "resource-challenged," and the like—but ultimately, we decided we had no use for euphemisms. Poverty is simply the condition of not having enough money to meet your daily needs. There should be no shame in using the word.

When we discussed the question of language with the families themselves, they agreed that there was no point in dancing around the reality of their situation. They were also quite specific about what they meant by "poor." "We're not poor of spirit," they told us in multiple ways. "We're not poor in ideas, or poor in determination. We're not poor of aspiration and we're not poor of dreams. It's just that we don't have the money to accomplish the things we want to accomplish. And sometimes we don't have the money to feed our kids. That's what being poor is. It's something you go through. It's not who you are."

This nuanced perspective is strikingly absent from the public discourse, where we either demonize all poor people as lazy and unworthy or divide them into the "deserving" and "underserving" poor. These narratives have tremendous political utility for those concerned with preserving the status quo. If people are poor because they are lazy, then the cure lies with them—work harder!—and no difficult social accounting or economic restructuring is required. If the poor *deserve* to be poor because of their own failings, then the rest of us must deserve our relative wealth. Money becomes a marker of personal merit, and our basic, human responsibility to one another is left by the wayside.

To acknowledge systemic poverty, on the other hand, means challenging the notion that those who have money work harder than the rest of us and are therefore deserving of all that they have. It threatens the myth of a classless society where anyone can rise with a little spunk and elbow grease. No wonder we'd rather stick with fairy tales featuring evil welfare queens and plucky kids who somehow "beat the odds."

At MCF, we work hard to counter this kind of reductive narrative. Above all, we aim through our communications work to elevate the voices of families. This is how you push back against dehumanization—by giving people a platform to assert their humanity and insisting that the nation pay attention. Until the day when we reach our larger goal of a nation where resources are distributed equitably and no family is forced to live in poverty, we will continue to push for a different story, one that reflects the experience of poverty from the inside out.

Chapter 6: Nurturing a Movement

From the depth of need and despair, people can work together, can organize themselves to solve their own problems and fill their own needs with dignity and strength.

—*Cesar Chavez*

Movement building permeates every aspect of the Marguerite Casey Foundation's work, from what we support to how we support it. If poverty is our target, movement building is the strongest arrow in our quiver. Given our limited resources and the vast scope of poverty in America, movement building is the best means we have to punch above our weight. It provides a powerful counter to the sense of isolation and powerlessness that goes hand in hand with poverty.

Finding our proper role as funders in this space has been a balancing act, one that calls for a mix of humility, flexibility, creativity, and hope. If our goal was to sow the seeds for a lasting movement, business as usual was not going to be adequate. It would not work to ask our grantees for top-down–defined deliverables and expect them to come back in a year or two with a report detailing how they had met them. If our intent was to empower a movement of low-income families speaking for themselves, it was essential that those families take ownership

themselves. The foundation had a role to play in catalyzing and convening this movement, but it did not fall to us to define, own, or lead it.

Focusing our grantmaking on movement building demands a level of patience that has been challenging for me at times. When it comes to change, my first instinct is to want it now. I have to remind myself that successful social movements unfold over a matter of decades, even generations. They certainly don't emerge within the constraints of a typical grant cycle. Making movement building the basis of a philanthropic strategy requires what I call "patient investment." We have to allow communities the time to develop rather than pulling our funding if we don't see the results we want within an arbitrary timeframe. As people begin to see their shared efforts spark change, their sense of their own potential expands. Over time, this sense of personal efficacy evolves into collective power, which in turn drives social change.

Movement building, I have come to understand, is cathedral building, because it calls on our better selves. It takes time and the work of many hands. By movement building, I mean more than just marches and rallies, although these can be important forms of expression. I mean tapping into low-income families' natural leadership potential and engaging those families every step of the way in changing policies to improve their own lives, the lives of their children, and the civic life of the community as a whole. With each grant we make, we remain mindful that as philanthropists, we are in service to our grantees and their constituents, rather than the reverse.

Our conviction that families must lead any movement that claims to represent them shapes every aspect of our work. It informs our strategy of trust-based investment: we provide organizations with long-term general support and trust them to know what to do with the resources we provide. This offers grantees both institutional stability and the flexibility they need to respond to events as they unfold. Movement building is messy, and opportunities may arise in a split second. General support enables grantees to pivot to face a new challenge or grasp a new opportunity without catastrophic challenges for the organization.

We knew going in that we were standing on the shoulders of giants. Individuals and organizations in low-income communities have devoted themselves to the task of movement building for many years. In most cases, these efforts have been fueled by "sweat equity" with little funding or formal infrastructure. We knew that money could never buy this kind of commitment, but we saw a clear role for foundation support. Organizing our work around movement building created a space for us in the field of philanthropy that was new and bold, that addressed the root cause of poverty rather than merely its symptoms.

Questions and challenges

Doing things differently in any field inevitably leads to challenges, and our own approach is no exception. MCF's mission, vision, strategy, and relationship with our grantees are novel in the philanthropic sector. Initially, this concerned some board members, who worried that the foundation's course of action could put us on the fringes of the philanthropic community. If other funders viewed MCF as an outlier, would they be attracted to support our grantees and our vision?

Nonprofits, for their part, were used to short-term programmatic support from funders, often within narrow issue areas. Some thought our promise of general support was too good to be true and were not yet ready to trust us as a partner. Others went too far in the other direction: they misread our commitment to long-term general support as an entitlement and stopped trying to raise money from other sources.

Inevitably, we made some mistakes in the beginning, investing in organizations that we later discovered did not have genuine roots in the community. A few responded to the notion of movement building by treating their base like a herd to be kept in line rather than as a source of leadership and power. Needless to say, these did not become long-term grantees. We were looking for organizations that saw their constituents as leaders, not merely bodies to turn up at a march. Over time, we were able to find these organizations, and today, they are the heart and soul of our grantee base.

Perhaps our greatest challenge to the status quo was our commitment to a movement and a grantmaking practice that eschewed silos. When we made this commitment, the word "intersectionality" had not yet entered the lexicon. "You need to pick," well-meaning colleagues and advisers insisted early on. "Focus on housing, or education, or child care; don't bite off more than you can chew." When I heard this, I thought of my own experience growing up. If someone had told my family we had to "pick" among the various challenges we faced—pay the light bill, or buy groceries, or take the kids to the doctor, but don't try to tackle all of these "issues" at once—I'm not sure what we would have done. We didn't have the luxury of choosing among essentials. MCF, I was determined, would not ask families to make impossible choices simply in order to streamline our own grantmaking.

The central paradox of organizing a philanthropic practice around movement building is the simple fact that movements are and must be driven by those most affected. To be of use, funders must relinquish much of what we have traditionally considered our role or our right. It is not for us to dictate goals or determine timetables. We can't dream up "special initiatives" and then expect those with the most at stake to organize their work for our greater glory. But as long as we remember that our role is to nurture, not to lead, I do believe that we as funders can ally ourselves with grassroots movements in highly effective ways.

Nurturing a movement

To understand MCF's commitment to movement building, we have to go back to the very beginning. Before we made a single grant, we commissioned forty papers from practitioners and thought leaders. The idea of nurturing a movement of families initially came from one of those papers. There were already enough dollars in the foster care system to do a better job of helping families succeed, the author argued, but that money was not being well spent. Only an organized, family-led movement could ensure the equitable distribution of dollars earmarked for the most vulnerable families. This was a pivotal insight for us.

Our commitment to movement building was further deepened by the Listening Circles that were the genesis of so much of our work. When we asked participants the question, "How would you leverage 30 million dollars a year to ensure the well-being of children, families, and communities?" they thought deeply and spoke from the heart.

Building public will, family members told us, required strengthening the ability of indigenous leaders to mobilize their communities for long-term action. "We want the best for our children and families, but we have little influence on the key institutions that impact our lives," they told us. "You don't have enough dollars to change those systems by yourselves, but you could help us learn how to be better advocates for our kids so that *we* could demand they be fixed." A look at history confirmed their analysis: only a large-scale grassroots movement led by those affected could move the dial on racial and economic justice in this country.

Personally, movement building had been on my radar for many years. Growing up in San Francisco, I saw the picketers outside of Safeway asking shoppers to boycott lettuce and grapes. Through them, I became aware of the movement Cesar Chavez and thousands of farmworkers were building to improve conditions for those growing and picking the food we ate every day. When Chavez went on a twenty-five-day hunger strike, losing thirty-five pounds and endangering his health, I was deeply moved. Until that moment, I had not realized how far people would go in order to make change, not only for themselves or even their own communities but for a universal principle such as equity or justice. Concepts that had seemed abstract when I learned about them in school became profoundly personal as I watched this man take himself to the brink of death in the name of justice. Across the country, Martin Luther King Jr. was putting his own body on the line in the struggle for civil rights. These movements made justice seem like a living, breathing thing—something worth fighting for, no matter the personal cost. If MCF harnessed our philanthropic resources to the power of grassroots movement building, it seemed to me, there was no limit to what we might achieve.

Even as MCF looked to the great movements of the past for guidance, we also understood the importance of looking toward the future. What would a twenty-first century movement look like on the ground? What were our goals, and what did we need to do differently to achieve them in this political and cultural moment?

The role of the church—so central to the success of the civil rights movement—had been largely supplanted by not-for-profits by the time MCF opened our doors. As social movements evolved from a religious base into a more secular, not-for-profit model, they also became more siloed, in great part because of the demands of funders. A professional leadership class developed, with executive directors who were well-trained and highly educated but did not always come from, or answer to, the communities in which they worked. These "grasstops" leaders were skilled at navigating the currents of political and cultural influence on behalf of the issues their organizations were concerned with, but they did not seem to have the deep connection to a base that is crucial to securing lasting change. Meanwhile, community members who, in past generations, might have looked to the church for leadership and moral direction did not always connect to the more secular community building efforts of the not-for-profits.

MCF addressed this shift in a number of ways. First, we sought out organizations that had a genuine grassroots ethos with priorities set and implemented by a broad and active base. We funded a number of smaller groups on whom others were unwilling to take a chance, organizations that may have needed some help shoring up their infrastructure but had the deep community connections on which movement building depends. We were also willing to take a chance when we saw potential for base building, even if it was nascent or incomplete, and provide the resources needed to develop it. Today, we are proud to support a cadre of long-term grantees that foster movement leaders motivated by genuine concern for their communities as opposed to professional ambition.

According to the National Committee for Responsive Philanthropy (NCRP), conservative funders had taken the lead when it came to organizing grantees into a political movement, in part by providing long-term general operating support, a crucial tool when it comes to movement building. This did not mean we should simply emulate the right. Conservative-led movements are often driven by funders' own priorities, not by any grassroots constituency, and NCRP researchers found that conservative philanthropies' successes had "resulted in policy decisions that have imposed a harsh and disproportionate burden on the poor." MCF was open to adopting strategies that had been successful on the right—most saliently, long-term general support—but we were committed to ensuring that families themselves retained control of any movement we supported and that any such movement benefited the nation's poorest families directly.

In April of 2004, we participated in a standing-room-only session on movement building at the annual convening of the Council on Foundations. When we presented our model, people thought we were crazy. "How does philanthropy build a movement?" they asked us with deep skepticism. Our answer was clear: "We don't." Movements are not designed in glass office towers by high-profile funders; they arise organically in response to a convergence of forces, led by those who have the most at stake. Foundations can certainly *invest* in social movements. We can support nonprofits and assist community members in their efforts to take part. We can bring people together to have conversations that inspire collective action. But all this is very different from "building" a movement. Only those most affected can build and lead a movement for social justice. History has taught us this again and again.

Criminal justice and the right to vote: a case study in movement building

If you asked me to name the greatest success I have witnessed over the life of the foundation, I would find myself hard-pressed to choose. Over the years, I have seen dedicated organizers and committed family members work together to change policy and practice on a wide range of issues of importance to their communities, from immigration to wages to working conditions to environmental racism and more. But in recent years, the scope of change on the criminal justice front has been particularly striking, making it a valuable case study in how those most affected, however powerless they may seem as individuals, can transform entire systems by working together within a movement framework.

In California, MCF grantees were part of a statewide coalition that pushed through the groundbreaking Proposition 47, which reclassifies a number of low-level drug and property offenses from felonies to misdemeanors. Its passage in November of 2014 meant early release for thousands of prisoners, kept thousands more from going to prison in the first place, and cleared the way for as many as one million Californians to strike old felonies from their records, opening doors to jobs, public housing, financial aid, and other essential opportunities. Making Proposition 47 a reality required a grassroots mobilization on a scale that is rarely seen. Thousands of volunteers contacted more than three hundred thousand voters and held more than two hundred voter-mobilization events. In addition to making Proposition 47 law, these efforts also spurred the development of a rapidly growing, tightly connected corps of family leaders who have a personal stake in the most pressing issues facing California and the nation and are ready for the next battle, and the one after that.

Elsewhere in states where we fund, MCF grantees have worked together to secure progress on due process, reentry, alternatives to incarceration, conditions of confinement, and much more. In Louisiana, parents of incarcerated children banded together with other activists to challenge that state's archaic and racially skewed juvenile justice system, securing reforms that culminated in a sweeping package of legislation in 2016. In San Francisco, formerly incarcerated activists launched a successful campaign to "Ban the Box," passing legislation that keeps employers from using old convictions to screen out job candidates. This grassroots effort sparked a nationwide shift. In 2015, President Barack Obama banned the box on applications for federal jobs, and by 2016, twenty-five states and 150 cities passed similar laws.

Most recently, I have been tremendously inspired by the movement that emerged around Amendment 4 to the Florida constitution, which restores voting rights to those with felony convictions. The right to vote has long been viewed as one of the highest forms of legitimacy, inclusion, and power in U.S. democracy. But prior to the passage of Amendment 4 in late 2018, nearly 1.7 million Floridians—one out of every ten adult residents—were barred from voting because of felony convictions, regardless of degree.

I first learned of the effort to change this in 2012 when one of our grantees introduced me to Desmond Meade. At that point, Meade was running the Florida Rights Restoration Coalition (FRRC) out of his home and car with no formal support. When Meade told me that people were being permanently locked out of the democratic process for offenses as minor as disturbing a shrimp trap or releasing a bouquet of helium balloons, I was appalled. At the same time, I was inspired by the fact that the Florida voting rights effort was being led by men and women who, like Meade, had been personally affected by incarceration. As Meade put it, "What we bring to this game is proximity to the pain. We're personally invested in it. How do we take the pain and transform it into purpose?"

Transforming pain into purpose takes resources, which MCF was honored to provide. "MCF allowed us space to fail," Meade said later, when the campaign had grown into a sweeping initiative with connections to virtually every community in the state. "It's hard to dream when you're afraid to fail."

When I see someone reaching out to people who have been disparaged and dismissed, inspiring them to engage in a political process from which they have been forcibly excluded, I see someone who is building a movement. That is what I saw in Meade. By fighting for voting rights for returning citizens, Meade was fighting for himself. At the same time, he was fighting for a voice for his community. Florida's history of shutting out black voters dates back to the Jim Crow era, when state lawmakers expanded the list of crimes that could disqualify someone from voting in an explicit attempt to keep black Americans from exercising their hard-won franchise. Prior to the passage of Amendment 4, nearly 25 percent of voting-age black people were disenfranchised in the state of Florida. This shocking fact has implications not only for those individuals but for democracy itself.

Amendment 4 organizers reached across race and issue in order to build their base, including developing a powerful black/brown alliance. They garnered support from immigration rights activists by pointing out that the same entities that were pushing for crime bills that fueled the overincarceration of people of color were also crafting anti-immigration legislation. As Meade memorably put it, "We grabbed hold of the narrative by the neck, and we shook it."

Specifically, Meade framed the right to vote as a family issue, pointing out that "those who don't vote are intimately connected to those who can't." In his youth, he remembered, voting was a family event. Everyone got dressed in their Sunday best and went to the polls together to exercise a hard-won right. But with so many black adults disenfranchised, all that disappeared, replaced by the kind of cynicism that is fueled by despair.

That was before an army of the disenfranchised hit the pavement. By January 2018, supporters had collected 1.1 million signatures to put Amendment 4 on the state ballot. MCF supported the effort with an unrestricted grant for nonpartisan voter and civic engagement efforts. This gave FRRC the flexibility they needed to open chapters throughout the state and hire returning citizens to do outreach work, including in communities of color. As FRRC political director Neil Volz put it, "Unrestricted funding is vital to building relationships that are the heartbeat of the movement."

As the Amendment 4 campaign gathered momentum, I was pleased to see other MCF grantees in the region join in. Equal Voice for Urban Florida, an MCF–supported network, drummed up support through its constituent base. New Florida Majority, Florida Immigrant Coalition, Catalyst Miami, Dream Defenders, and Organize Florida held town halls, ran Get Out the Vote campaigns, registered voters, and reached out to constituents in immigrant communities. On November 6, 2018, Amendment 4 won with 64 percent of the vote, making it the largest expansion in voting rights in the United States in nearly half a century—passed at one of the most divisive moments in our country's history. Now, the powerful coalition that evolved around it is poised to continue working together to advance a broad range of criminal justice reforms.

"What would be so powerful that it would cause people to put aside political differences and racial insecurities to come together for a common good?" Meade asked after the victory. Based on what I witnessed, the answer is movement building: that magical alchemy that turns insight into action and love into power. Whatever you call it, the Amendment 4 experience only deepened MCF's commitment to nurturing similar efforts across our grantmaking regions.

Supporting the fight for voting rights in Florida aligned with MCF's larger commitment to funding Integrated Voter Engagement (IVE), which we see as crucial to building political power in underrepresented communities. Unlike traditional Get Out the Vote efforts, IVE programs remain in place year-round, building power and sustaining impact over multiple election cycles. Community members trained to conduct voter engagement efforts become the infrastructure for civic engagement and community organizing, which in turn grows the base for the movement. It is predicted that by 2065, the eligible voting populations in twenty states, which together account for almost two-thirds of the country's population, will likely be majority-minority. In this context, efforts to make the electorate more inclusive are essential to the larger fight for racial and economic justice.

The struggle for voting rights is only one facet of a multi-issue movement that is taking root across the country. Nothing is more rewarding than hearing grantees speak of their work collectively, using "we" to mean not merely their own organizations but themselves as a collaborative, or hearing a family member describe his engagement with a particular campaign or network as "an act of love." We are fostering a movement that, already, has grown far beyond us—seeding work that cannot be undone, because it is held in a multitude of hands.

Chapter 7: The Equal Voice Campaign

A movement happens when people from across an area start thinking the same way, understanding the issues the same way, and understanding the solutions the same way. I think that is what's happening with Equal Voice.

—Patricia Van Pelt, Illinois state senator

On September 6, 2008, thousands of family members poured off buses and out of cars in Birmingham, Alabama; Chicago, Illinois; and Los Angeles, California. Babies draped in blankets slept on their parents' shoulders while giddy older siblings dashed through hotel lobbies and road-weary parents shared hugs and greetings. Hotels accustomed to solo business travelers lit up with the boisterous energy of children and families. The eighteen-month Equal Voice for America's Families campaign—sponsored by the Marguerite Casey Foundation but driven by our grantees and their constituents—was drawing to a close, and participants flooded into conference halls for three linked national convenings where they would ratify a national family platform that would communicate their concerns and solutions to the world.

I attended the Birmingham convening, where a burgundy-clad mariachi band greeted new arrivals with guitars, violins, and accordions. The conference hall quickly filled with talk and laughter as families poured in, eager to meet or reconnect with one another. I stood back and marveled at what I saw before me and on massive screens bringing simulcast images from Los Angeles and Chicago: the ideals on which MCF was built reflected back to me in the weary, hopeful faces of family members from all over the country who had traveled many miles in the hope of being heard.

MCF chartered two hundred buses, booked eight hundred airline tickets, and reimbursed mileage for hundreds of passenger cars to bring fifteen thousand people together for the national convenings. Linked by simulcast and joined by another five thousand online viewers, the group voted to endorse the National Family Platform organized around eight core areas of paramount importance to families: child care, education, criminal justice reform, employment and job training, health care, housing, immigration reform, and safe and thriving communities. Representing the shared vision of families across the country, the platform contains policy recommendations at the local, state, and federal levels.

The Equal Voice campaign was a manifestation of the foundation's mission, but it was also a test. If we gave families the chance to come up with solutions to the most pressing issues they faced, to link their voices and demand to be heard, would they take it? The answer, I saw as I looked around me in Birmingham, was a resounding yes.

I have given more speeches than I care to count, but the wave of adrenaline that swept through me as I faced the crowd in Birmingham was something new. "Today, we have come together to change the world," I told those assembled. "Yes, to change the world. And it starts here, today. *Si, se puede!*"

"*Si, se puede!*" thousands of voices sang out in reply.

Then I introduced Brandon Mitchell, a black father from New Orleans who had struggled to keep his family afloat in the wake of Hurricane Katrina. "One thing I have learned from this campaign is that my struggle is connected to other people's lives across the country, and that we need to come together as one, regardless of racial and ethnic background," he told the rapt crowd. "If we haven't learned yet to accept one another for who we are, we're not going to be accepted by any government to make the changes that we need. We are the people. We are the voice. And what *we* need is what matters most."

"*Si, se puede!*" the crowd cheered again. Yes, we can.

Manifestation of a mission

Like everything we do at MCF, the Equal Voice campaign was driven by the voices and imperatives of our grantees and the families they represent. In 2006 and 2007, we hosted a series of convenings in each of our grantmaking regions. One of the ideas that came out of these gatherings was the formation of a Movement Building Study Group. Comprised of representatives from thirty-four grantees, the study group would meet periodically to advise the foundation on movement building strategy. In 2007, we held a Movement Building Study Group Retreat in Atlanta, Georgia. Among our goals was to plan some kind of event that would bring families together to identify their most pressing concerns.

Attendees listened respectfully as I shared my vision for an event: a large-scale, one-time gathering of families that would inspire grantees to greater collective action while helping to shape

MCF's future efforts as well. Then, just as respectfully, they vetoed it. A single convening, they told me, wasn't going to do it; they wanted a campaign, not merely an event. They envisioned town halls in every region where MCF made grants. What came out of those gatherings, they decided, should do more than inform the foundation's work, or even their own. They had their eye on the next presidential election. The Democrats and the Republicans would each be putting forth platforms, but if history was any guide, the needs of poor families were unlikely to be central to either. Those in attendance at the study group meeting thought we should come up with something of our own—a national platform that would ensure that family voices were heard over the din of campaign promises and competing political agendas.

When MCF first began discussing the prospect of a national campaign, we hoped to engage perhaps five thousand families. As interest and momentum grew, we allowed ourselves to imagine as many as ten thousand coming together. But the effort grew in unexpected ways. Targets were met and then exceeded again and again. By the end of the eighteen-month campaign, we counted at least fifteen thousand family members who participated in sixty-five town hall meetings and another fifteen thousand who gathered at the three simultaneous, digitally linked national convenings to ratify the Equal Voice National Family Platform. In the best way possible, the campaign had gotten out of our hands and into those of the families themselves.

In Chicago, MCF grantee Rami Nashashibi, the director of that city's Inner-City Muslim Action Network and now an MCF board member, attended the national convening with Imam W. Deen Mohammed. A son of the Nation of Islam leader Elijah Muhammad and a prominent leader in his own right, Imam

Mohammed was known for his racially and religiously inclusive vision. After the event, Rami shared with me the imam's strong reaction to what he had witnessed. "I never thought I would live to see this day," said the imam, who was in his seventies then and had spent a lifetime battling the legacy of segregation and trying to unify diverse and sometimes embattled groups. What struck the imam most, Rami told me, was the profound sense of unity he had experienced at a radically diverse gathering that included people of every race, religion, and background. "He had been in interfaith settings," Rami said, "but had never seen that type of organized power and possibility among communities who had often been on the losing side."

I shared the imam's sense of awe and amazement. Even though I had been involved in every step of the planning process, there was an emotional resonance to the national convenings that swept me off my feet. From the beginning, MCF had organized our work around a vision of racial justice and unity that went far beyond standard "diversity initiatives." The great majority of MCF's board, staff, and grantees are people of color. At the national convenings, I saw our vision of multiracial leadership writ large. "Seeing this many people of color, from so many cultures, it feels like we've passed the test that our civil rights leaders fought for," one participant told me as the Birmingham convening drew to a close. "It's like the dream is happening."

"We want change and justice"

The Equal Voice campaign represented a grand experiment for the foundation and our allies. Since our inception, we had organized our work around a commitment to movement building as the bedrock for broad and lasting change. Now, in partnership with our grantees and their constituents, we would test that commitment at a national scale. How far could we advance our vision at a moment when our country was more diverse than ever in its history but also more economically stratified?

Our goal was to bring together the efforts we had seeded across the country into a unified, national family movement. The movement we envisioned would recognize families as repositories of solutions to their own concerns and make enough collective noise to press these solutions onto the national stage, where poor people, if they are considered at all, are more likely to be talked about than heard from directly.

The challenges before us were significant, but we also had tremendous assets going in: our grantees and their constituents. Reflecting a diverse array of communities and aims, they shared a core belief that families have the capacity not only to describe their own struggles but to identify solutions. This made them a natural base for the ambitious endeavor that was Equal Voice.

We also faced some serious obstacles. The Equal Voice campaign coincided with the Great Recession—the most severe economic meltdown the country had experienced since the Great Depression. The unemployment rate reached a high of 10 percent, reflecting an increase of 8.6 million in the number of people out of a job. Forty-six million Americans did not have health insurance. Millions more faced a daily struggle to provide food and shelter. As we traveled the country holding meetings and town halls, the U.S. economy was unraveling around us.

Foundation endowments plummeted along with the stock market. Many funders dialed down giving and, in some cases, suspended grantmaking altogether. Nonprofits were hit hard:

a Nonprofit Finance Fund survey found that nearly a third did not have more than a month's operating cash on hand. But even as our own endowment plummeted, MCF found ways to maintain our commitment to our grantees. We adjusted our grant-making timeline, making two-year grants rather than three, but we did not reduce the level of funding at a moment when we knew our grantees, and the families they worked with, needed it most.

Through the Equal Voice campaign, we stepped up our efforts to engage directly with as many families as possible. In partnership with 250 grantee organizations in twelve states, we held a series of sixty-five town hall meetings, starting with a group of men incarcerated at Monroe Prison in Washington State. Listening to these men talk about how parenthood anchored them to the fate of their communities—even as they were locked away from those communities—was profoundly moving.

So were each of the gatherings that followed. In churches, coffee shops, and community centers across the country, we heard from parents, grandparents, and youth. Their words provided an urgent call to action:

> *I'm sinking more and more, because I'm working as hard as I can, and it feels like I'm not getting anywhere.*
>
> *I've seen three people get killed on my block. It was drug violence.*
>
> *Families are getting desperate, because they can't provide for the children.*
>
> *We want change and justice and fairness. We want equality.*

We heard the desperation in the voices of parents who worked multiple jobs but still struggled to meet their children's basic needs. At the same time, because the campaign brought us into the homes and lives of families, we also had the chance to see hidden strengths: the sustaining force of familial reciprocity, the buoying effect of laughter and simple affection. I think often of Brandon Mitchell, who was raising three small children on his own after his family had been scattered by Hurricane Katrina. Their struggle to rebuild felt nearly overwhelming. But watching Mitchell's young son pick out the tune to "Twinkle, Twinkle, Little Star" on his guitar to lull his little sister to sleep as the family snuggled together on a mattress in their temporary home, I was reminded of the strength and comfort I drew from my own family in the years after we too were dislocated and had to rebuild our lives in an unfamiliar place. These moments of connection strengthened my commitment to ensuring that voices like Brandon Mitchell's were heard on the national stage.

"Your voice in this process is crucial," we told families at every opportunity. "Without it, we don't have a campaign." Participants responded with an overwhelming appreciation for being perceived as capable of changing their own futures. They also found tremendous value in being connected with others from around the country who shared their struggles and their sense of urgency. I will never forget the image of a young grandmother with a baby on her hip and her fist in the air, leading the crowd in a spontaneous chant: "We have nothing to lose but our chains!"

Breaking barriers, making connections

It was 36 degrees in McAllen, Texas, but hundreds of families braved the cold and poured into the huge white tents we had raised for the town hall. Some had no coats, but they came all the same, gathering in small groups to identify the issues that were most important to them, then marking their top priorities with colored dots. Children put puzzles together in the corner while their parents brainstormed in the next tent over. In the children's open, hopeful faces, I saw a vivid reminder of exactly what it was we had gathered to fight for.

"I always believed that families like you could create a blueprint for change for this country," I told those assembled in Spanish, their native language. "Those dots on those sheets on the wall represent the beginning of that change."

"No one has ever asked me to share my point of view," one of the participants told me later. "Thank you for doing that."

During the eighteen months of the campaign, I spent countless hours in conversation with families. They told me about the pressures they faced day to day, but they also spoke of the energy they drew from participating in the Equal Voice endeavor. Along with the sense of agency that came from being responsible for setting campaign priorities, many said that the process itself—listening to others tell their stories and feeling emboldened by that experience to tell their own—made them feel less alone in their struggles. That sense of solidarity made them trust their own voices in new and powerful ways.

For me, this was one of the most moving aspects of the campaign—hearing from people across the country as they tested their voices and plumbed their collective power. Anton Charles, a young man I met in Chicago, described his involvement in the campaign as life-changing. "It's hard to believe there's an organization that would actually value a teenager's opinion," Charles told me, looking up from the notebook where he was mapping out plans and ideas in a hurried longhand. "The Equal Voice campaign values your opinion no matter what age and no matter what race, and no matter what anything you are."

Charles was nineteen when he joined the campaign through Chicago's Albany Park Neighborhood Council. "In all other aspects of life, you have people just working—just getting by," he said after a particularly lively planning meeting. "These people at this meeting were trying to make a difference, trying to change things, to make life better for others. I felt like since I was a part of it, I could do the same thing."

In many ways, the Equal Voice campaign was the greatest challenge I faced in my first decade at MCF. At the leadership level, it sometimes took hours of face-to-face wrangling to get erstwhile rivals to sit down together and find common ground. Over time, however, these struggles gave way to moments of connection and mutual understanding among people who had not had the opportunity to sit down together—much less work side by side—before the campaign. It moved me deeply to watch as an African American father struggling with the consequences of a criminal conviction realized that an undocumented Mexican worker was not an "outsider" impinging on jobs that should rightfully be his but rather a parent like himself, trying to feed a family despite backbreaking legal barriers and the constant fear of arrest.

This was just one of many ways in which the Equal Voice campaign gave us the opportunity to watch our values play out on the ground. The importance of cross-issue organizing, for instance, was thrown into relief as organizers accustomed to focusing on jobs came to understand, through direct interactions, that people could not work if they did not have housing, green cards, child care, or bus fare. These insights led to new and lasting alliances among organizers working on issues they might previously have seen as unrelated. Over time, these connections wove a net that would carry the weight of the hopes and aspirations of the tens of thousands who participated in the Equal Voice campaign and the many more they represented.

The eighteen months I spent crisscrossing the country, from the desert mesas of New Mexico to the snow-covered streets of Chicago, were among the most memorable of my tenure at MCF. At some of the town halls, the diversity ran so deep that we heard a dozen languages spoken in one room (we offered simultaneous translation via headset). Although we used technology to enhance connectedness at every opportunity, the heart of the effort was face-to-face work in conference rooms, living rooms, and church basements across the country. Those who might otherwise have been divided by race, region, issue, or ideology broke bread over tables strewn with markers and butcher paper as they worked together to hash out a platform they all could stand behind. In the process, they discovered the depth of their own commonality. Again and again, participants told me of attending a town hall or planning a meeting and discovering that "the other" was, in fact, just like them—in their experience, their struggle, and their aspirations for their children and community.

The commitment to keeping families at the forefront of the campaign, not as spokespeople or showpieces but as leaders and decision makers, was central to the Equal Voice effort. Old habits die hard, from reporters accustomed to interviewing executive directors rather than working parents to those directors themselves, who sometimes struggled with ceding power to those they were more accustomed to representing. But moments of friction were the exception. More often, the dedicated activists and organizers who staff and run our grantee organizations expressed deep appreciation for the opportunity to connect with one another and return to their movement roots.

During the campaign, the Center for Community Change worked alongside us to document the ideas coming out of the town halls and organize the data by issue. In June of 2008, we brought fifty campaign participants to Chicago to look at what had emerged and weave it together into a coherent platform.

If ever I needed proof that families had the capacity to seize their own destiny, this gathering provided it. The families in attendance had such a deep understanding of policy and such zeal for capturing one another's ideas—they were writing on the walls, debating at the tables, and brainstorming in the hallways with unflagging energy. They took great care in teasing out the best way to categorize issues within the platform and also paid close attention to what might be missing. "What about the youth?" they asked. "Are the elders taken care of?" I had never seen people so deeply engaged in articulating policy that reflected their communities' values and needs. In turn, several people told me they had never felt so deeply heard.

We at MCF did our best to make the conversation possible, but beyond that, we were hands-off: the platform belonged to the families. We took the same approach to financing the whole endeavor. MCF paid for everything necessary to make town hall meetings and other campaign events possible—transportation and hotels for the families, food, child care, posters, brochures, translators—and hired nine regional coordinators to help weave together local efforts. This approach fostered cooperation among grantees, who shared resources in order to advance common aims rather than competing for them. We also made sure grantees knew that they would not lose MCF funding if they chose not to join the campaign. This made the level of engagement we saw especially gratifying. Although participation was entirely voluntary, and no organization received direct funding for participating, 95 percent of our then-250 grantees chose to join the Equal Voice campaign.

Through the Equal Voice experience, family members came to understand that they had a role to play in improving the systems that affected their lives. At one town hall after another, people who might previously have felt invisible or unrecognized shifted their perspective as they saw their own struggles reflected in each other's. Strangers turned into allies. The relationships forged over hot coffee at the start of a long day, or lukewarm coffee as a group continued its work long into the night, laid the groundwork for continued collaboration. This, to me, was the heart of the campaign: the shared meal, the spontaneous conversation, the flash of connection that, again and again, inspired those involved—myself included—to delve more deeply and advocate more vigorously for a family agenda grounded in shared experience and fueled by a powerful sense of common cause.

Every issue is a family issue

In the months following the Equal Voice campaign, the recession deepened, throwing families into turmoil across the country. In 2009 alone, 3 million people lost their jobs. Even as we celebrated the success of the campaign, the recession forced us to ask difficult questions. Had Equal Voice crystallized into a genuine social movement of and for America's poorest families? If so, what would it take to sustain that movement over the long haul, even as the families at its center struggled to keep their heads above water?

Clearly, the eighteen months of intensive community and campaign building across the country had generated a tremendous amount of energy and emotion. People who had never before had an opportunity to weigh in on the national stage found not only their individual voices but also a sense of solidarity that few had experienced before. If that had been the end of it—if we had simply gone out on the grace notes of the national convenings, writing up the final reports and resting on our laurels—the good will and collective energy we had built together over those eighteen months might well have soured into cynicism. Those involved could easily have been left thinking that this was "just another foundation initiative," undertaken for our greater glory, only to be abandoned when an arbitrary deadline was met. But this is not how movements work, nor is it how MCF does business. The campaign itself was intended to be time-limited, but the platform that came out of it was not. Instead, it would guide our work for years to come.

In 2009, family delegates from twelve states hand-delivered the platform to forty-two senators and representatives in Washington, D.C., and released it to the public at the National Press Club. It was a powerful experience, but we also learned some hard lessons about the intransigence of power. I remember joining two of our grantees, both black women, as they went to deliver the platform to their state senator. He stepped out of his office, took one look at them, and said, "I don't represent you." Then he turned on his heel and retreated into his office. I had never experienced anything quite like it. I thought public officials were required at least to *pretend* to be responsive to their constituents, but he didn't even feel the need to do that much.

After the campaign wound down, we saw participants themselves seek ways to continue to work together to promote the platform and pursue common aims. These relationships conveyed to us that we had succeeded in building lasting bridges among disparate groups. They also offered a blueprint for the foundation's future. Risky as it was, the Equal Voice campaign had become a determining inflection point for us. Its ultimate success validated our larger philosophy and deepened our commitment to "Ask, Listen, Act."

In October of 2009, we hosted a follow-up convening in San Francisco to discuss ways to advance the aims of the platform beyond the parameters of the eighteen-month campaign. As I mingled with the three hundred individuals in attendance, I marveled at the strength and commitment that led them to keep fighting, knowing that many were struggling in a spiraling economy. "It's been a rough year," I acknowledged when the time came for me to address the group, "but we have a linked future. We belong together, and we will change society."

Grantees and their constituents shared the tools to do exactly that. They learned how communities could benefit from federal economic stimulus dollars; participated in a workshop on using media as an advocacy tool; and generated a list of future actions they planned to take together to advance the platform. For me, the highlight of the day came when participants spontaneously began chanting, "Every issue is a family issue."

Polling done during that gathering indicated that despite the economic pressures of the past year, the momentum generated by the Equal Voice campaign was growing. Since the national convenings, more than two-thirds of participants polled had contacted elected officials, built coalitions, volunteered, and/or connected with others in their communities around the Equal Voice platform. Many groups had hosted gatherings of their own, from small strategy sessions to multiday conferences. Several were using a "report card" framework to measure progress on the platform issues and hold policymakers accountable.

In 2012, we hosted online gatherings in Louisiana and Texas, where family members reviewed the platform again and gave it their endorsement. By then, MCF was using the platform to structure our grantmaking around the concerns that families had identified as most urgent. The Equal Voice campaign had functioned as a living laboratory for our young foundation, testing our values and revealing which strategies were most effective in bringing people together around a common aim. As then–Southern Echo Executive Director Leroy Johnson put it, the time had come "to move from just crying in the wilderness to developing a plan that will make our lives better."

In the wake of the campaign, we celebrated our successes, studied our failures, and—most importantly—made plans to incorporate the relationships and strategies that had come out of it into our future work. For eighteen months, we had organized ourselves around a single question: if you give them a chance, will families unite across barriers in pursuit of a common aim? The response had been a resounding "yes." This gave us the fuel we needed to drive our work forward.

Chapter 8: Linked Futures

The movement of the next century is a networked movement.

—"Connecting the Unconnected," proceedings paper, MCF 2004 working session

In 2016, the Marguerite Casey Foundation had our version of a *quinceañera*, a fifteenth birthday celebration that marks a young woman's coming of age in many Latin American countries. We launched this landmark year with the first-ever statewide convening of California grantees, a three-day gathering in San Diego that harnessed the power of more than one hundred grassroots advocates.

Convenings have always been a central part of MCF's movement building practice, but as with so much else, we do them in our own way. We try to avoid the trap of traditional funder-led gatherings: high-status, low-impact events that bring small groups of "thought leaders" to foundation headquarters for a single meeting with no mechanism for sustaining new relationships or implementing new ideas. Instead, we invest in frequent gatherings that serve as a jumping-off point for low-income families to come together with grassroots organizations and gain the critical mass to advocate on their own behalf. These convenings also strengthen our Equal Voice Networks—working collectives that bring grantees together to build relationships and advance shared aims across a spectrum of issues.

The San Diego gathering brought together members of all four of the state's Equal Voice Networks, with representatives from the Central Valley and San Diego joining the more established Bay Area Equal Voice Coalition and the Equal Voice for Southern California Families Alliance. California is at the forefront of America's shifting demographics—59 percent of the state's residents are people of color, and nearly half the state's children have an immigrant parent. California is also an epicenter for civic engagement. Across the state, foundation grantees are working together within the network framework to advance every issue on the Equal Voice platform.

Against the backdrop of a contentious election year, which was marked by hate-filled language and images of fistfights along the campaign trail, those at the San Diego convening engaged in face-to-face conversation about how to work together to knock down barriers of race, class, and immigration status. In meeting rooms, hallways, and under the sun on the expansive hotel terrace, participants asked questions aimed at fostering alliances and advancing movement building:

> *"How can we support each other?"*
> *"How do we build power?"*
> *"What is the next step?"*

For me, the most valuable aspect of these gatherings is the opportunity they afford me to interact informally with the family members who make up the heart of our work—people like Craig Roberts, whom I found sitting at a conference table sporting a baseball cap that read "Straight Outta Skid Row." Craig once worked on commercial airplanes as a Lockheed employee, but for nearly twelve years, he had been living on Los Angeles's Skid Row, where residents complain of police harassment and fourteen thousand homeless people were arrested in 2016 alone. He was there with fellow members of the Los Angeles Community Action Network (LA CAN), which operates under the motto "House keys, not handcuffs." "I live the experience," Craig said, explaining why he had come to the convening. "I want to be part of the real fight."

As Saturday morning unfolded, participants spilled into conference rooms lined with blank white paper. Using colored markers, they outlined their goals for the year ahead. "Collaboration is essential," wrote a member of the San Diego–based Center on Policy Initiatives, summing up a key theme of the gathering. Attendees discussed a range of shared aspirations: better educational opportunities, environmental justice, curtailing gentrification and displacement, improving public transit, reforming criminal justice, upholding human rights for the LGBTQ community, fighting police brutality, and creating access to affordable health and child care. They also discussed ways to work together across issues, with the goal of improving families' lives.

A multiracial planning committee of community leaders from each of the four regions in the state had organized the convening around an agenda designed to build collective power and advance policies that would meet the needs and reflect the dreams of California's families. My role at the event was to welcome and, most of all, to listen. As I did, I could feel in my bones what it means to be in alliance. The event was a much-needed counterpoint to the fear and isolation many of us were feeling in the midst of that troubling campaign season.

At one workshop, Shonda Roberts, an Oakland, California, fast-food worker and leader in the movement to raise the minimum wage, described the moment she realized that she was not alone in seeking a better life for herself and her children. It was at a labor meeting, she said, where she saw hundreds of other fast-food workers before her. They, too, were ready to fight for decent wages and better opportunities so families could thrive. In San Diego, the other advocates in the room soaked up her words. They asked questions and relayed experiences from their own communities. When it came time to wrap up for lunch, the group was too energized to stop. "We don't want lunch," Shonda said, to laughter and agreement. "We want to keep talking." By the time the regional meetings gave way to a statewide discussion on Sunday, common goals had emerged, with an emphasis on voter empowerment, civic engagement, and youth leadership development. There was talk of increasing the minimum wage for the entire state and addressing property taxes so more dollars would be available for education.

Alicia Garza, special projects director at the National Domestic Workers Alliance and a co-founder of the Black Lives Matter movement, spoke of the burgeoning national movement for racial justice. "We believe we stand on the shoulders of giants, and some of those giants are in this room," she told the audience, who responded with a standing ovation. "We need to focus on building power."

I am always pleased when grantees develop strong relationships with the foundation, but that is an internal metric. When grantees tell me that MCF has helped them to strengthen their relationships with one another, that is when I know that our strategy is succeeding, because it is these on-the-ground relationships—manifested as networks, convenings, or even shorter-term, single campaign alliances—that have proven, again and again, to spark change.

Coming together

Today, the seventeen Equal Voice Networks that exist across the country are so deeply woven into the collective work of the foundation and our grantees that it is hard to imagine how we would function without them. Like many lasting relationships, it all began with the breaking of bread.

More specifically, the networks were launched over plates of spit-roasted goat in Reynosa, Mexico, a city of six hundred thousand on the southern banks of the Rio Grande river, just across the border from McAllen, Texas. Today, the region has become a flashpoint for the debate over immigration, with President Donald Trump visiting McAllen to warn of the dangers he sees looming across the river and push for his border wall. Back in 2005, we were just looking for someplace to eat.

We'd begun our formal exploration of network building the previous year, when we convened theorists and practitioners from across the country for a wide-ranging brainstorming session with foundation staff. Starting from the understanding that—as Marty Kearns of Green Media Toolshed wrote in a paper for the session—"social change will require an engagement of a connected web of people, organizations, agencies, foundations, and businesses," we asked the group to identify mechanisms for supporting networks that would respond to the demands and visions of low-income families while amplifying their power and collective voice.

That conversation ranged widely, as guests shared insights from mathematics, physics, anthropology, computer science, and more into how networks function and what they can achieve. We looked to existing networks for models, but our aim went beyond simple replication. The challenge I issued the group was to identify ways to connect the most disconnected people in America. My hope was that, over time, these networks would nurture and develop the power that lay latent within low-income communities while uniting these communities with one another.

This initial brainstorming session was valuable, but also— with its charts, graphs, and academic language—a little too abstract. In its wake, I decided that the most efficient way for MCF to figure out how best to connect people was simply to do it: to bring people together and see where that took us. That is how a group of Latinos from Texas and African Americans from Mississippi wound up sharing rice, beans, and roasted goat in an out-of-the way restaurant in Reynosa.

By that point, MCF had identified the Mississippi Delta and the Rio Grande Valley as promising sites for movement building efforts. Both regions were home to community groups with strong track records of engaging families, but both also struggled with deeply entrenched poverty. Something had to change in these often-neglected regions, and we saw bringing people together as the first step.

The idea behind the networks was not only to mobilize families but also to connect regions, races, and ethnicities—in this case, the primarily black residents of the Delta with the predominantly Latino families of the Rio Grande Valley. I had long been aware of the forces that divide black and brown Americans and keep us from acting on our many common interests, and one of my goals in supporting networks was to build bridges between these two groups.

We had not planned on an international excursion, but when Maria Reynaldo, who was working for us as a consultant at the time, said "Let's take them to Reynosa," it seemed like the perfect way to start things off. We parked by the river and made the border crossing on foot because we wanted people to experience what it feels like to walk across an international border. Part of building a relationship is gaining a direct understanding of the other, and conversation can only take you so far. There are times when you have to experience something in order to understand it.

When it comes to building lasting relationships, especially cross-culturally, I am convinced there is no substitute for sitting down together over a leisurely meal. When I was growing up, my whole extended family would gather at my grandmother's each Sunday for a meal of *gallo pinto*, a rice-and-bean dish widely eaten in Nicaragua. I remember the first time I brought my now-husband Bill. I had told him so much about our wonderful Sunday dinners, and I think he was a little disappointed when he saw what was on the table. "It's just rice and beans!" he said. "What's the big deal about this *gallo pinto*?"

By the end of the meal, Bill understood. It wasn't what was on the table that mattered but everything around it: the care that went into preparing the food, the shared effort and nonstop conversation. Looking back, I see that my own family really did function as a network. We called ourselves *los lobos*, and that's what we were—a wolf pack. Whatever we did, we did it together.

Networks have something else in common with families: they pose a challenge to the deeply American notion that if you want to be successful, you have to get there on your own. I remember being shocked the first time I heard the term "codependence" used in a pejorative way in this country. Codependence was a way of life for me! I depended on other people to help me survive in this country. I depended on other people to help me with my child. I depended on them for transportation. To this day, I depend on my family for support. I depend on them for joy! What some call codependency, I call connectedness. Whatever you call it, it is not a mental illness. It is a tremendous source of strength and power.

As soon as our group made it into Reynosa, we turned our attention to finding a place to eat. We had about thirty people to feed, but eventually we found a place that was able to accommodate us. Roasted goat was a first for many at the table, but everybody ate, and everybody talked. That meal marked the beginning of a long-running conversation that continues to this day.

Our excursion did have its disheartening moments, as we realized that racism was alive and well on both sides of the border. As we wandered into souvenir shops selling kitschy sombreros and miniature guitars, shop owners who had never seen so many black people in one place became visibly nervous. At the restaurant, the owner kept a watchful eye on us throughout the meal. Rather than letting these tense moments go by without comment, we used them as a launching place for an important conversation.

Our next step was bringing the Latino contingent on a civil rights tour of the American South. We began that leg of our journey by visiting a prison notorious for forcing black men into hard labor and ended it eating barbecue and dancing to the blues in a small town in Mississippi. The whole point of these trips was to build relationships. As black and brown people living in America, we shared so much in common, yet we were so often pitted against one another. Why, I wondered, did we fall prey to these forces of division when we could achieve so much more by working together?

As participants visited each other's towns and cities, they began to see beyond old divisions to shared concerns and strategies. By trading stories on the road or over meals, people from different backgrounds came together, found common ground in their legacies and life histories, and drew from that the motivation they needed to work together more closely.

The first two formal networks grew out of these early gatherings. Drawing on what we had learned at the 2004 brainstorming session, we hired "network weavers" (a term coined by June Holley, an Appalachian organizer) in the Rio Grande Valley and the Mississippi Delta. These network weavers would be charged with helping to build and strengthen relationships among grantees and increase their collective capacity. To nurture trust and collaboration within and across the two regions, the foundation brought the fledgling networks together at a convening in McAllen, Texas, in 2006.

This gathering was rich with meaningful conversations, but one in particular stands out in my memory. Douglas Patiño, a founding MCF board member and lifelong warrior for racial and economic justice, was speaking with nonprofit leader Helen Johnson, who is African American. Johnson had been asked to chair a meeting of blacks and Latinos in the South, and she was worried about her ability to steer the conversation. "I don't know anything about Latinos," she acknowledged with the kind of courageous honesty that marked those early conversations. Douglas, who is Latino, immediately offered his help, but he also offered crucial reassurance. What mattered, he told her, wasn't what she *already* knew—it was her willingness to jump in and learn more.

This conversation and others like it would ultimately inspire us to launch the Patiño Moore Legacy Award. Given in partnership with the Association of Black Foundation Executives and Hispanics in Philanthropy, the award recognizes organizations whose work fosters collaboration between Latino and African American communities to effect change for all of America's families. The award is named after Douglas Patiño and Wenda Weekes Moore, both leaders in the fields of higher education and public service, for their work to improve relations between black and brown communities. Each year since 2011, we award 150,000 dollars to selected organizations to recognize and support their ongoing work.

This award is meaningful to me because it reflects our commitment to connecting people across race in an intentional way. At the same time, it memorializes the openness of spirit that guided us during those formative early years when we were forging the connections that would grow into the networks.

From outrage to action

Initially, the networks focused on building relationships and trust among members. Once that trust was established, members identified a project or projects on which to collaborate—creating fairer legislative districts, for instance, or increasing funding for neighborhoods and schools—and created working groups that reflected their shared priorities. As longtime Rio Grande Valley network weaver Michael Seifert puts it, "The rules that work for the network are the same rules that would work in a healthily functioning family: mutual respect and an explicit understanding that [different] people do things differently."

If Equal Voice Networks are the mortar in a family-led movement, the network weavers are its masons. Network weavers help members identify mutual interests, share information, and strengthen relationships to expand their collective impact. It is a broad and subtle role that covers everything from setting meeting times to establishing priorities. Sometimes, a network weaver's most important job is getting members in the same room on a regular basis and then simply listening. As Chicago network weaver Ed Shurna puts it, "You don't take this job because you want to become known. If you're always trying to make sure that your star is the brightest and your name is at the top of the list, you're not going to create a successful network."

The most successful network weavers grasp a lesson that has informed MCF's work since our inception: effective leaders are also followers. Sometimes they take the opportunity to speak, but most of the time they are listening, learning, guiding, and supporting. Rather than seeking personal glory, network weavers draw inspiration from those around them. In their day-to-day work, the network weavers embody the foundation's promise to "Ask, Listen, Act." They have to walk gracefully among multiple perspectives while at the same time helping to unite network members behind concrete activities. Their job, as one network weaver put it, is to help "bridge the gap from outrage to action."

In recent years, I have noticed increasing interest in network building within the larger philanthropic community. This is good news. At the same time, I am aware that MCF's approach to networks is unusual, if not unique in the field. Funder-supported networks are generally affinity groups brought together by shared interest or a commitment to a particular issue. MCF takes a different approach. Rather than encouraging self-segregation, Equal Voice Networks serve as a mechanism for cross-pollination.

By participating in non-issue based networks, organizations are exposed to new strategies that may not yet have penetrated their particular field. Participants gain insight into the connections among issues, which fosters a deeper understanding of the multiple, intersecting challenges poor families face. Most crucially, by forging and sustaining alliances across boundaries of race, place, issue, and ego, networks help build the critical mass necessary to create broad-based change.

The rich diversity and deep cooperation I see today among the Equal Voice Networks is one of the foundation's singular achievements—all the more so because it is hard won. Many of the networks struggled at the beginning, some for several years. There were times, especially in the early years, when I sat in on network meetings and nearly wept with frustration as I watched dedicated activists fail to find common ground.

This failure, I came to see, was due in great part to the way philanthropy traditionally operates. Because so many funders require adherence to strictly delineated program areas, nonprofit leaders had grown wary of working together outside familiar boundaries. As they struggled to figure out where next year's budget or even next month's payroll would come from, potential allies too often wound up seeing one another as competitors for scarce resources. By asking grantees to work together in networks, MCF is asking them to share power. When organizations are in competition for funding, this can be challenging.

No network weaver, no matter how gifted, could solve these conflicts on his own. What has ultimately made the Equal Voice Networks successful is a combination of the weavers' talents, members' good-faith efforts, and MCF's unique funding model. Over time, long-term general support shifts the power dynamic on the ground. By neutralizing fear and rewarding collective engagement, it allows grantees to continue doing their own core work *and* work together at the same time. As grantees have come to understand MCF's approach and trust in our support, they have grown increasingly comfortable with collaboration. By strengthening their partners, network members understand, we make their own work stronger. In a competitive funding environment, this is a profound shift.

As California network weaver Donna Bransford has put it, multiyear general operating support gives grantees a break from "the hamster wheel of 'I gotta get the next grant, I gotta get the next grant.' The kind of grants that MCF makes gives them a little breathing room so they can spend some time thinking about 'What do we actually need and how are we going to get there?' Then the network is a table where there are relationships with people who are asking the same questions and have the space to engage together and imagine a bigger vision."

Investing in relationships

While the first MCF–supported networks preceded the national Equal Voice campaign, the connections made during that campaign created tremendous momentum, and the networks expanded rapidly in the years that followed. Working together, grantees discovered through the campaign, allowed them to access one another's skills, power, and base to achieve far more than they could alone. On the foundation end, we saw how supporting collaborative action could produce exponential returns on both foundation investment and the time and energy of grantees. By investing in relationships, we are not only building social capital, we are creating the conditions for this intangible asset to compound, just as we aim, through wise fiscal stewardship, to compound our financial assets for maximum social impact.

From 2009 to 2012, the foundation capitalized on the energy the campaign had generated with a series of mini-grants intended to solidify the infrastructure for lasting collaboration by strengthening and expanding on the network model. The strategy proved effective. In the months and years after the Equal Voice campaign formally wound down, we saw signs all around that the momentum it had generated was growing rather than dissipating. Coalitions blossomed within and across our grant-making regions. Promises to stay in touch led to "what's next" conversations and a collective rolling up of sleeves. Most crucially, the Equal Voice Networks took off, so that today they number seventeen across the country. Together, they have racked up an impressive number of wins.

In Los Angeles, a network of twenty groups gathered under the Equal Voice banner to continue the work they had started during the campaign. Using the National Family Platform as a template, the Los Angeles network devised a cross-issue report card to assess local government on issues such as education, employment, public safety, and immigration. They organized convenings of their own and met regularly in smaller groups to develop strategies for addressing those issues families had identified as most pressing. In what had become the MCF modus operandi, the twenty diverse groups worked together across issues, driven by the shared concerns of the families they represented. At a time when many nonprofits were facing budget cuts because of the recession and could easily have seen one another as competitors for a shrinking pool of funding, this kind of partnership was especially striking.

In Chicago, the Equal Voice campaign helped spur the development of the United Congress of Community and Religious Organizations (UCCRO), which brings diverse groups together to move a local agenda closely aligned with the National Family Platform. Patricia Van Pelt—a co-founder of UCCRO who is now an Illinois state senator—has said the campaign "helped us to bind ourselves together with another knot." Through the networks, she observed, the foundation's vision of "having low-income people understand that they have a role to play in decision making that impacts their lives" was beginning to take hold across the nation.

"People have become informed and willing to speak up for themselves and understand that they're not alone," Van Pelt elaborated. "There are people struggling all over the nation, and people all over the nation are saying, 'We deserve better, and we will have better, because we're going to fight to get something better.' I think that's a movement—a movement to empower low-income families with the ability and the space to speak on their own behalf and make decisions about the laws that govern their lives."

In 2009, when the foundation released the first of three

requests for proposals designed to support networks that had formed or grown stronger during the Equal Voice campaign, we were thrilled to receive more than fifty proposals from collaboratives drawn from our 250 grantees—local, regional, and national nonprofits that work with families in the poorest areas of the country. The networks we subsequently funded worked to advance issues and strategies highlighted during the campaign while remaining grounded in the diverse communities their members represented.

In Marin County, California, a network that had originally come together to plan a town hall evolved into the Equal Voice Leadership Academy, which aimed to build family capacity to move local and regional issues. An Atlanta network focused on providing training in clergy-specific organizing methodologies to African American pastors. These trainings in turn energized a group of young pastors to support parent networks working to improve public education. We supported these emerging networks with grants intended to solidify the infrastructure for lasting collaboration, but then we stepped back as the networks determined their own aims and activities. By moving power to families, networks flip a traditional relationship in philanthropy. Instead of telling grantees and families what to do, the foundation provides infrastructure support and opportunities to convene, but the networks themselves set priorities and determine action.

Those involved with building these networks told us they found great value in being connected with other like-minded, like-situated people from around the country. Through these connections, they came to see that the challenges they faced were not unique to their family or community but were part of larger economic struggles taking place across the country. There is a tremendous power that comes from this realization—a sense that collectively, network members can tackle forces that, faced alone, appear overwhelming.

The success of the networks was so striking that it convinced us to move from a policy of encouraging grantees to work together under the umbrella of a network to requiring that they do so as a condition of funding. As we bring in new grantees, the network lens has become an important metric. Is a particular organization open to the kind of cross-issue collaboration an Equal Voice Network entails? Will it bring an approach or strategy from which other network members can learn? Grantees that are not interested in working collaboratively are, over time, replaced on the docket by groups that welcome the opportunity.

While we are always cognizant that the role of the foundation is to convene, not to lead, we also recognize that networks do not simply happen on their own. They require time, staffing, and resources—hard to come by for nonprofits that are struggling to maintain their own programs and campaigns. This is why MCF has increasingly used our resources to invest in network infrastructure.

Initially, the foundation paid the network weavers directly, and they reported to us. As part of our ongoing effort to transfer power to those doing the work, we changed that in 2012. Now, the networks hire their own weavers, and the weavers report directly to the networks. Institutional shifts such as this may seem symbolic, but we believe they are crucial to promoting autonomy among our grantees and shifting the traditional balance of power.

Key wins and campaigns

The clearest sign of the power of networks to spark change is, of course, change itself. Across the country, hundreds of thousands of low-income families have mobilized as part of Equal Voice Networks to win higher wages, criminal justice reforms, improvements in health care, LGBTQ rights, better schools, fairer immigration policies, and more. Each new victory strengthens bonds, refines strategy, and helps lay the groundwork for the next. The result is that over the last decade, Equal Voice Networks have helped win everything from affordable housing in Chicago and better schools in the Mississippi Delta to reduced prison sentences in California and more inclusive census counts in the Rio Grande Valley.

In Chicago, that city's Equal Voice Network leveraged a 50,000-dollar voter engagement grant to build grassroots support that resulted in then–Mayor Rahm Emmanuel redirecting 88 million dollars to the city's public schools. Network members also used the campaign as an opportunity to educate parents about other community issues, including the critical need for an elected school board to represent their interests.

The Louisiana Equal Voice Network/Power Coalition for Equity and Justice developed a statewide People's Agenda that included raising the age at which children can be sentenced as adults, implementing Medicaid expansion, and developing policies that protect the LGBTQ community. A big win came in 2015 when the state legislature adopted Raise the Age legislation. The Louisiana network also worked with New Orleans–based organizations on a campaign that helped usher in the Hire NOLA ordinance, the city's first worker participation program. In a city where 44 percent of working-age black men were unemployed, the program examined barriers blocking black men from jobs and connected job training to employment. In 2016, New Orleans responded by instituting a policy that requires contractors to ensure that at least 30 percent of all work hours are performed by local workers and at least 10 percent are performed by disadvantaged local workers.

In California, the four regional Equal Voice Networks have helped advance a living wage, stem the school-to-prison pipeline, ease re-entry for those leaving prison, halt unfair evictions, and advance equitable housing in the region with the highest rents in the nation. California network members successfully organized to raise the minimum wage at the local level, then moved on to the state level, convincing then–Governor Jerry Brown to increase the statewide minimum wage in April 2016. California networks have also made a concerted effort to engage potential voters, with the Equal Voice for Southern California Families Alliance reaching a record 10.3 million via get-out-the-vote activities in 2016.

California grantees have also provided crucial leadership to three regional electoral alliances: Oakland Rising, San Francisco Rising, and Silicon Valley Rising. The three combined to form Bay Area Rising, which has become a powerhouse in coordinating efforts to win local initiatives. The "Rising" alliances have been central to moving the dial on minimum wage and tenants' rights initiatives in multiple Bay Area cities.

The ability of networks to elevate the collective power of families and organizations extends beyond MCF grantees. The national Native Voice Network has thirty members, less than half of whom are MCF grantees. When the Native Voice Network organized a national call-in to pressure FedEx over its association with the NFL's Redskins franchise in Washington, D.C., it mobilized both grantees and non-grantees, ultimately reaching over one million people. Hundreds of individuals, organizations, and tribes agreed to boycott FedEx for its continued sponsorship of the team. When FedEx distanced itself from the team, it showed members that together they had power.

These victories have not come without challenges. Turf issues have flared, power struggles simmered, and personal conflicts emerged as activists accustomed to competing for scarce resources gradually learned that they could *be* resources to one another. But nothing builds trust like shared work and shared wins. Today, just as they are most needed, the networks we support are battle-tested and ready to take on the challenges ahead.

Together, the networks have the capacity to create a collective voice for poor families that is loud enough to be heard above the bellowing and posturing that have come to characterize political culture in the United States. As longtime organizer and current MCF board member Rami Nashashibi put it in the wake of the 2016 election: "We're ready, because we have already been in these fights together. We've had our disagreements, and we've learned to work them out. We know one another, and we know how to work together."

Chapter 9: Race, Gender, and Philanthropy

When you try to stand up and look the world in the face like you had a right to be here, you have attacked the entire power structure of the Western world.

—*James Baldwin*

I had not been in America long when, as a new immigrant, I embarked on what would prove to be a lifelong education on the relationship between poverty and race in this country. It started the moment I walked through the doors of San Francisco's Mission High School. Finding myself assigned to one of the most under-resourced schools in the city, I looked around and saw only black and brown faces staring back at me. Everyone looked like me, and everyone was poor. There's an understanding that comes with that realization. On a personal level, it comes as a big, hard slap in your face. You realize how little people expect of you in this country once they see a brown-skinned face—how much harder you'll have to fight for every shred of opportunity. That's a lot for a teenage girl to absorb. But absorb it I did. The brutal intersection of race and class in my new country was something I would come up against again and again in my own life and throughout my career.

Because race and class *are* so deeply intertwined in this

country, the battle for equity must focus on both racial and economic justice. But people are still very uncomfortable talking about both race and money in this country. The taboo that forecloses any real discussion of racial injustice is just as powerful as the one that makes it so hard for us to have an honest conversation about poverty. For more than three decades, I have been advocating for diversity and inclusion in the field of philanthropy. And for more than three decades, people have been telling me to quiet down.

I can't tell you how many times I've had to have one version or another of the same conversation. I remember being on the committee for an event at the Council on Foundations. I suggested as a speaker the great Mexican writer Carlos Fuentes. I'm sitting next to these two very liberal guys, white men, both highly respected in the field, and one says to the other, "Wow, all she talks about is Latino issues." Eventually, I disengaged from that particular process. Sometimes you get tired of fighting the same fight.

My personal background—as an immigrant, as a woman of color, as someone who has experienced poverty firsthand—has made me the "only one" in so many of the rooms I have entered in my professional life. At first, you feel your difference, and the isolation that comes with it, quite acutely. Over time, you grow accustomed to it and start to develop coping mechanisms. Then, as your career advances, you are thrust into new environments and forced to defend yourself and your perspective all over again.

Working in this field as a woman of color requires a balancing act every single day. As a Latina in a largely white field, I've grown accustomed to being expected to be the expert on all things Latino, then being shut down when my voice is perceived as too much or too loud. "What are you complaining about, Luz?" colleagues will ask when I express my fatigue at constantly being the "only one" in the room. They point to my own success as evidence of equity or trumpet small shifts in the number of people of color in philanthropy. The subtext, sometimes made explicit, is that my concerns are unwarranted, or at least exaggerated.

How do I explain to them that justice is more than a question of numbers—that justice demands a shift in values as well? If you don't hold racial justice in the forefront of your values, if you don't exercise those values on a daily basis, if you don't speak truth to power, then you don't have anything. *We* don't have anything.

Time's up for tokenism

I find myself in the position of "only" not only because of my race but also because of my gender. The field of philanthropy may be largely female, but at the leadership level, we disappear. The first Latina to lead a major national foundation, I remain to this day one of a small number of women of color in similar positions within this field. Yet people are constantly crowing about "progress," instructing me to be happy with things as they are. "Look at the changes that have taken place," they tell me. "Look at yourself! Here you are in a leadership position." Then they'll point to someone else in a similar position, without thinking about what it means that they can count us on one hand.

I have worked hard to make my way to the place where I now stand, and at the same time I acknowledge my good fortune. But calling myself "lucky" and leaving it at that begs an important question: why, after all these years, do I still find myself one of a handful of people of color in so many rooms where decisions about us are debated and made? Am I supposed to sit quietly in these rarefied spaces—to pretend I don't notice my own exceptionality? I can't do it, and I won't do it. I'm not going to sit there like a plant, just for color, my name on the program but my voice silenced. It's like being invited to sit at the table but not allowed to eat.

This kind of tokenism has gone on far too long. It's time to correct it. The only way to do that is for those of us who are treated this way to speak out. We need to call people on it, no matter how uncomfortable that makes everyone in the room. Otherwise, it's never going to go away. I don't enjoy being seen as "the angry Latina," but I'll weather the stereotypes if that's what it takes to open the door for others—to ensure that we are heard as well as seen in the rooms where decisions that matter get made.

Sometimes I get impatient—I've been fighting the same battle for so many years—but I remind myself that real change is measured not in years but in generations. I may not ever see the kind of deep equity I've fought for throughout my career, but I am determined that my grandchildren will. Looking at their faces, filled with the hope and idealism of the young, helps keep me going, even when progress is painfully slow.

And let's face it: change *is* slow. We've been talking about diversity and inclusion in philanthropy for decades now, but the fact remains that fewer than 8 percent of foundation trustees are people of color, a reprehensibly low figure (by contrast, 80 percent of the Marguerite Casey Foundation's board members are people of color). Even in the somewhat more diverse nonprofit field, according to BoardSource, fewer than 20 percent of executive directors are people of color.

Year after year, I see young people of color enter the field full of passion and ideas. They want to make a change. But time after time, I watch them become disheartened as they discover that there is no room for the change they envisioned. Instead, *they* are expected to be the ones to bend—to compromise their principles in order to accommodate themselves to the imperatives of their employers. They find themselves caught between the community they come from and this new one—the philanthropic community—they are trying to join. It's a hard place to find oneself in and a harder place to stay.

So when my colleagues in philanthropy talk about the need to diversify the field, I have to ask them: what are *you* willing to give up? Are foundations willing to change to accommodate the voices and perspectives of multiple cultures, or is the expectation that those individuals of color who are granted entry to the field will be the ones to change? Is the field truly open to new ideas or just new faces spouting the same old rhetoric?

Sure, I can look around me today and see a handful of other people of color in leadership positions at major foundations. And yes, I am proud of what we have achieved. But after years and years of talk about equity and inclusion, we still don't have the influence we should have in terms of how programs are designed; how communities are invited to be part of that process, or not. Things may have changed for the better over the years, but "better" is not equity. "Better" is not justice. So I continue to speak out, even at the risk of being seen as a provocateur, trying to remake this field in the image of its own stated values. At the same time, I challenge the notion that making these changes should be the responsibility of people of color only. The burden of history, of poverty, of racial injustice, is the responsibility of all of us in this country, and until we all share in shouldering that burden—starting with simply being willing to speak up— we will not see the kind of progress that justice demands.

Changing the narrative

As does anyone, I brought my personal experience with me when I came to MCF. I knew in my bones how it felt to be the only one in a room—the impossible expectations that are placed on your shoulders when you're forced to play that role—and I was determined not to replicate that model by asking anyone else to stand in for an entire community. How do you avoid this all-too-common practice? The only way is through an unshake-able commitment to diversity in the deepest sense of the word. No tokens. No half-measures. No empty promises.

This was the commitment we made when we started MCF: that we would seek diversity and practice equity not only in who we funded but also in our staff and on our board of directors. As I look around me today, I'm proud of what we've achieved. Eighty percent of the members of MCF's board of directors are people of color, and over one-third are women of color. The majority of our grantmaking team are people of color as well. This is highly unusual within philanthropy. Even foundations that profess to value racial equity, and that primarily serve com-munities of color, rarely have a board or staff that resemble those they serve. In 2017, BoardSource surveyed 141 foundations. They found that "foundation boards lack racial and ethnic diversity in profound ways—and current recruitment practices demonstrate that is unlikely to change." Among the foundations surveyed, an average of 85 percent of board members were white, as were 95 percent of board chairs and 89 percent of CEOs. Forty percent of foundations surveyed had boards that were 100 percent white. Most troubling was the finding that nearly one in five chief executives reported they were not prioritizing demographics in their board recruitment strategy, despite being dissatisfied with their board's racial and ethnic composition. These findings make MCF's demographics all the more striking.

At MCF, our board and staff mirror our constituency directly. I am immensely proud of this fact, but equity doesn't end at the foundation door. Who we are matters only to the extent that it shapes what we do. We need a diverse staff who can connect with the communities we serve, not so we can create a pretty, multiracial brochure but so we can make the best grants possible. The backgrounds and experiences MCF staff and board members bring to the work matter because they inform the decisions we make about how best to allocate the foundation's assets.

Our commitment to internal diversity is intimately related to our larger commitment to building a multiracial, cross-issue movement for justice. This is where the rubber meets the road at MCF. Eighty-six percent of our grants go to organizations that are led by people of color, and the great majority serve communities of color. Women of color lead more than half our portfolio. We also go out of our way to seek out vendors that are run by women or people of color. Every aspect of how we show up in the world is deliberate and has been from the start. We are driven by the core value of the Diversity, Equity, and Inclusion movement within philanthropy: that in order to make good grants you need a diverse staff that can reach out to the communities where the on-the-ground work is happening.

The kind of top-to-bottom diversity that MCF practices doesn't just happen. Maintaining a commitment to equity requires stepping outside your comfort zone and reaching beyond those you know or who come recommended by people you know. That kind of insider hiring only perpetuates the status quo. Nor is it enough to appoint a "diversity committee" that meets bimonthly to bemoan the same old problems, or to soothe your conscience by launching "special initiatives" aimed at communities of color. At MCF we don't crow, "This is our women-of-color initiative!" Instead, the values of diversity, equity, and inclusion are integrated into all aspects of our work.

These same values shape every aspect of our grantmaking philosophy. By making long-term investments in smaller, often lesser-known groups with a leadership and a constituency of people of color, for example, MCF is changing the field more than we ever could through a time-limited diversity initiative. The truth is, our goal is far more ambitious than simply "diversifying" our grantee base. We aim for nothing less than to make the dream a reality. That means 85 to 90 percent of the grants going to poor communities of color—the communities most in need of movement building support. It also means pushing our collective work across the lines that have traditionally divided communities and hindered movement building. Race is central to that effort because race is at the very heart of movement building. We are working within a tradition that is grounded in the struggle for racial justice in this country.

Priming the pipeline

In 1979, when I was still at the Irvine Foundation, I went to my first meeting of the Council of Foundations. I remember walking around with my eyes wide open, looking for other Latinos. From what I could see, I was by myself. Finally, I went through the registration booklet looking for Spanish surnames. There were a total of two. I called them both.

The first woman became brusque when I told her why I was calling. "I am a Spaniard," she told me imperiously. "I am not a Latina. And really, I am not interested in talking to you."

The second woman was polite but apologetic. "I'm sorry," she said, "I'm just married to a Latino."

So there I was. I could either accept that I was going to spend my career as an exception, or I could try to do something about it. That's why I started Hispanics in Philanthropy (HIP) to find a voice for Latinos in the field. As a first step, every time I received an annual report from a foundation anywhere in the country, I went through it line by line, trying to identify other Latinos working in the field. I'd call total strangers, introduce myself, and say, "I just came from the Council on Foundations, and I didn't see many Latinos. I think this field needs a Latino voice. Do you have time to get together?"

I came up with about five people to start with. We began meeting and trying to figure out what it was we could do together. We set out with a very simple notion: how do we help and support one another? We tried to create a forum, a space for Latinos to talk to one another and build solidarity. Over time, we became more ambitious: what can we do to diversify the field?

In 1983, we decided it was time to incorporate. We had a lot of aspirations, but we faced real challenges as well. As individuals (most of us were the "onlies" at the foundations where we worked), we had no power within our own organizations. So then the question became: "What can we achieve together"? How do we break past the fear and get to the point where we could actually change things? All the while, this small network was becoming the support group for the single Latino at more and more foundations. Slowly but surely, we were building strength in numbers.

HIP became an important part of my life. It sustained me in this field. What makes me especially proud is knowing that it has done the same for so many other Latino professionals struggling to find a toehold within philanthropy. Miguel Bustos, a longtime colleague who serves on the board of HIP, remembers what things were like when we started the organization: "If you were black, brown, or red, you were out in the streets organizing. You never saw people who looked like you or came from a similar background sitting on a foundation board." If you want to change the demographics of how money is spent, Miguel has pointed out, you have to change the demographics of who is empowered to disperse it. This is where I feel both HIP and MCF have broken new ground.

My commitment to racial justice extends beyond individual or group self-interest. MCF is a proud member of the Executives' Alliance to Expand Opportunities for Boys and Men of Color, a group of about forty foundations that are working on building an infrastructure to support black men and boys. We are also proud to have been recognized in a recent report from BMA Funders as one of the top ten foundations providing support to black men and boys. Through our Patiño Moore Award and many other efforts, MCF also works to improve black/brown relationships and combat the forces that would play us against one another.

Because we are so attuned to the relationship between racism and poverty, our commitment to diversity and inclusion goes beyond race. We are always seeking new ways to include those with firsthand experience of poverty in our work at a leadership as well as an advisory level. In 2012, we launched the Sargent Shriver Youth Warriors Against Poverty Leadership Awards, which annually recognize a select group of young activists from a pool of nominees submitted by grantee organizations. In 2016, we invited all past and present "Shrivers" to apply for the new Pat Schroeder Board Fellowship. This fellowship offers a Shriver Youth Warrior the opportunity to participate in MCF board meetings for an eighteen-month term. The fellowship creates the opportunity for a young activist to develop leadership skills, increase awareness of board governance, and broaden knowledge of social justice and movement building. At the same time, the board fellow adds a youth perspective to board matters. Ultimately, we hope this effort will contribute to the development of a pipeline of philanthropic leaders with a more diverse range of backgrounds and experience than the field currently reflects.

The same goal inspires MCF's participation in the Momentum Fellowship program, which Philanthropy Northwest launched in 2015 to bring people of color into the field of philanthropy. The fellowship offers participants work experience, professional development, mentoring, and networking opportunities. Moreover, it offers MCF and other participating foundations a rich source of talent.

Integrating the value of racial equity into every aspect of our work requires a dedicated practice of listening. We have to work hard to hear people's issues, both grantees and staff, to include everyone in the practices that we develop both internally and externally. Sometimes this requires having uncomfortable conversations. But today, nearly two decades in, we can proudly say that we have evolved into a high-end model of diversity, equity, and inclusion in the field of philanthropy.

Chapter 10: Power Together

Power without love is reckless and abusive, and love without power is sentimental and anemic. Power at its best is love implementing the demands of justice, and justice at its best is power correcting everything that stands against love.

—*Martin Luther King Jr.*

"Watch out," cautioned a friend with long experience in the field of philanthropy when I began my tenure as president and CEO of the Marguerite Casey Foundation. "Once you control a budget, you'll never have a bad idea again, or a bad meal. Don't let it go to your head!"

Her warning was apt. Take on a leadership role within philanthropy and your head may never stop spinning. Your calls are returned instantly, your most trivial ideas are received as if they were revelations, and people who were asking you to bring them coffee not long ago are now asking if you take one sugar or two.

The adulation that comes your way when you have money to disperse can be intense and intensely distorting. The power you wield as a funder can make it difficult to have genuine conversations or form authentic relationships. This undermines the work rather than advancing it. I don't ever want to become so sure of my own vision that I become immune to the wisdom of others. So, when people tell me I "don't act like a CEO" because I gather, reflect, listen, and share with people, I choose to take it as a compliment.

If I let the power that comes with my job go to my head, I realized early on, it would stand between me and my deepest aims. Philanthropic leaders need to remember that we don't have all the answers. We must learn and work together with our grantee partners to cocreate solutions. But breaking through established hierarchies to create this kind of partnership is no small feat. It takes patience, vigilance, and most of all humility.

The most important thing MCF has done toward mitigating the power gap is to eschew issue-based funding and offer long-term general support. If you can set up a system of checks and balances to make sure you protect the resources of the foundation but leave the decision making in the hands of those doing the work, you've gone a long way toward shifting the balance of power.

Making a grant and then moving out of the way is not something that comes naturally to funders because it requires giving up control, but that is exactly what makes it so important. The way I see it, the funds in our endowment already belong to the community. Our responsibility is to get the money out the door in the most effective way possible—to build power in the community, not hoard it for ourselves.

Foundation staff are not the only ones who sometimes have trouble stepping back so others can step forward. Nonprofit leaders can also find power-sharing challenging. In the early years, some struggled with the bottom-up nature of the foundation's approach. A few longtime leaders chafed at our insistence on engaging directly with constituent families rather than following the more familiar model of interacting only with directors and select staff.

Whenever we hold a convening, we ask each grantee to include a community member in their delegation. During the Equal Voice campaign, one of our grantees sent a staff member and a constituent to a meeting rather than attending herself. This was fine with me, but later on, once it became clear that we were actually setting policy priorities at this particular convening, the executive director called to chastise me. "Luz," she scolded, "if I'd known *this* is what you wanted I'd have come myself. I'm just not sure the families can tell us what they need."

Most people won't put it quite so bluntly, but the truth is, it can be difficult to get those in the upper echelons of nonprofit leadership to trust in those they claim to represent. At another convening, I watched as the executive director of a parent training organization sent the young man accompanying her to ask me a question. I answered as fully as I could, expecting that my response would open a dialogue between us, but he simply thanked me and went back to stand beside the director, who smiled at him as if he were a favored child. In this moment, it was clear to me that she was not genuinely building community leaders—an enterprise that requires giving up some personal power.

A commitment to community power requires more than rhetoric. It demands that those who, whether we recognize it or not, are accustomed to exercising a certain amount of power come to terms with sharing that power so that those most affected can find space to lead. The work begins with listening, but it doesn't stop there. Over the years, MCF has come up with a set of strategies that allow us to scrutinize all of our practices through the prism of power. To begin with, we strive to build authentic, lasting, honest relationships with our grantees. More importantly, we work to create the space for grantees to build lasting relationships with one another and the communities they serve. These ground-level relationships form the infrastructure for movement building.

Too often, funders use the power of the purse to force grantees to change gears in order to keep up with whatever issue area happens to be in vogue at that moment. This is profoundly counterproductive. Program-specific funding is movement building kryptonite. It promotes silos, diverts staff time away from core efforts, and fragments the work on the ground. At worst, it can cause funder-driven mission drift. In order to remain effective, community-based organizations must be accountable first and foremost to their constituents. When funders flex our power via narrowly defined program areas and time-limited "special initiatives," we risk forcing community groups to fit their work into the boxes we have drawn rather than attending to the needs their constituents have expressed. When we trust local leaders to know what is most needed, grant dollars feed directly into empowered communities. This is the kind of power MCF aims to build.

When we were trying to help build a national Native network, we hosted a convening of Native leaders at the Pueblo Art Center in Albuquerque, New Mexico. When the meeting started, they unceremoniously kicked me out of the room. I was overjoyed. The fact that these indigenous leaders felt comfortable claiming their own space without fear of losing the foundation's support let me know that we had succeeded in sending the right message. Since then, grantees have politely dismissed me from one meeting or another on several occasions. These moments are meaningful to me because they tell me I can trust those I'm working with to tell me the truth, whether or not it is what I want to hear.

Mission vs. ambition

"The narcotics of power are a quiet, near-ubiquitous poison," strategic philanthropy guru Hal Harvey has written. "A real foundation leader must ensure that the program staff does not succumb to the poison."

At MCF, we determined early on that in order to inoculate ourselves against this poison, we had to re-envision the role of the program officer. In a field where arrogance and high-handedness tend to increase with every zero on a check, we were determined to establish a different way of doing things. As Ruth Massinga, our first board chair, put it many years ago, "Every job needs to be filled not just with someone good but someone who wants to *do* good over a long period of time."

This job description has served us well over the years. The widely held notion that program officers should be hired based on their subject matter expertise misses the mark. Grantees themselves are better positioned than any funder to offer expertise on the needs of their communities. We don't need to dispatch "expert" program officers to step in and tell them what their constituents need or how best to provide it. Instead, what we look for in a program officer is expertise in relationship building and the capacity to approach the work with humility and respect.

This value drives not only our hiring practices but also the way we structure the job of the program officer. An individual program officer at MCF does not carry a traditional portfolio. Instead, program officers work together from a shared pot to determine the final distribution of grant funds. This means grantee organizations do not have to worry about shifting priorities, nor about "their" program officer being replaced by someone who may not have the same vision. Each MCF grantee's long-term relationship is with the foundation itself.

While we don't divide program officers by issue area, we do assign each to a specific region. This allows them to build lasting relationships with a group of activists who are simultaneously building relationships with one another, all of which fosters the collective work of movement building. Instead of focusing on a single issue, program officers are able to immerse themselves in the region they serve. They understand that there is only so much we can know sitting here in our office in Seattle. The real action is taking place on the ground.

At its best, our unusual approach to grants management creates an atmosphere of collaboration rather than competition among program officers. Unfortunately, it can also create the perception among ambitious program officers that there is insufficient room to grow their own careers within the foundation. Program officers who aspire to ownership of a particular portfolio, or who hope to rise within a hierarchy by attaining leadership of a specific program area or initiative, may find adapting to MCF's collaborative approach challenging.

There have been times when an individual's desire to make a mark via new grants or initiatives clashes with the foundation's commitment to providing long-term support to cornerstone organizations. These moments are difficult, but at the end of the day, our greatest obligation is to those on the ground, fighting each day to advance a family movement even as they struggle to feed their own families.

When conflicts arise between mission and ambition, I remind my staff that the money we are tasked with disbursing does not belong to us. We didn't earn it, we don't get to keep it, and we aren't the ones who are doing the work. The job of a program officer at MCF is to act as a link between resources and people who are making movements happen, not to make those people jump through hoops to obtain essential resources while doing the back-breaking work of creating social change.

Philanthropy is a demanding vocation, and those who come to it are often motivated by the love of humanity that defines the field. At the same time, philanthropy is not without its seductions. Too often, I have watched as even the most dedicated program officers become dazzled and distracted by the attention they receive from grant-seekers and grantees. Remaining true to our conviction that families are the experts on their own lives requires a generous dose of humility. When we speak of the need to work across barriers of ego and status, we are talking to our grantees but also to ourselves. We must hold ourselves to the same standard we ask of them, even when it causes frustration among passionate professionals who hope to advance agendas or strategies that, however worthy, distract from our central mission.

MCF's approach represents a profound departure from the traditional balance of power within philanthropy, and making it work for all involved has been one of the greatest challenges of my career. I am constantly trying to identify people who are genuinely committed to family-led movement building and who understand the importance of surrendering institutional power so that people can lead. Most of our program officers share this commitment and succeed in resisting the temptations that come with access to money and power. Nevertheless, I can think of too many instances when I have watched in dismay as dedicated program officers got distracted by the ego rewards that come with the territory.

It is certainly painful to watch talented program officers move on because they need the ego satisfaction of bringing their own set of grantees to a foundation or having unilateral control over a budget. But those moments are the exception. Far more often, I am privileged to witness the evolution of a different kind of program officer, one who understands that her main job is that of relationship builder and trusted ally to the dedicated nonprofits that make up our grantee base. These relationships lead to a kind of job satisfaction that runs far deeper than the ego rewards often associated with the field. Those who seek credit may find themselves disappointed, but those who seek transformation will find themselves deeply rewarded.

At the end of the day, what I see when I look around the MCF office is not ego but heart. Not long ago, I walked by the office of a member of our team and saw that she was in tears. She had just gotten off a call with Senator Patty Murray's office about the family separation taking place at the border and was staring at a photo of a breastfeeding child being pried from her mother's arms. These images and events are agonizing for all of us, but I draw comfort from the fact that we have built an organization rich in people who care deeply about one another and about the suffering in the larger world.

Family is more than a buzzword at MCF. My colleague, herself

a mother of three, wept because she felt the pain of this mother
and child in her own skin. That kind of empathy filters into the
work. It keeps us honest at the deepest level, fueling our work to
build a family movement and buoying my own spirits in times of
struggle or disappointment.

Power together

Even as we exercise great caution when it comes to our personal
power as funders, we are determined to build a different kind
of power: what I call "power together." Unlike the "power over"
reflected in traditional hierarchies, power together derives from
the collective strength of individuals and communities working
together toward common aims.

We saw this value in action in May of 2016 when we brought
together a group of young activists to build power through a network of their own. A spirit of possibility infused the MCF office
as these emerging leaders gathered to share their varied histories
and plan their collective future. All were past or current recipi-
ents of MCF's Sargent Shriver Youth Warriors Against Poverty
Leadership Award. While many foundations have a soft spot
for "grasstops" leaders, giving the same fellowships to the same
degreed and credentialed experts year after year, we take a different approach to cultivating leadership. By asking community
organizations to nominate candidates for the Shriver award, for
instance, we are able to find natural leaders already working in
communities across the country.

Crystal represented the Chicago Coalition for the Homeless,
which she joined after her mother's death left Crystal homeless
herself. Alejandro flew in from Tennessee, where he worked

with the Tennessee Immigrant & Refugee Rights Coalition in the fight to halt the deportation of young "DREAMers"—youth who had come to this country with their families as infants or small children and now sought the documents they needed to study, work, and build lives for themselves. Facing the threat of terrible consequences, the DREAMers still find the courage to speak their truth to power. They remind me that we are all human beings, whether we have the papers to prove it or not. Together, we have the ability to demonstrate that humanity and to demand that others respect it.

Now, Crystal, Alejandro, and their fellow Shrivers were coming together to explore the ways in which their various struggles were intertwined and discover the power they might draw from working together. As the conversation migrated from MCF's conference room to local coffee shops to the roof of our building and back again, the group listened eagerly as each spoke of the issues that drove them, from a living wage and immigrant rights to school reform and ending youth homelessness.

Crystal had been living on the streets for four years when she connected with MCF grantee the Chicago Coalition for the Homeless, which helped her find low-income housing. Like many of the community members who work with our grantees, she came through the door looking for help but emerged with something more: a sense of her own power. When she first came off the streets, Crystal told the group, "I thought 'OK, I'm housed, I have an apartment on my own, I'm safe,' but still I had the mindset that this was too good to be true. I had to work on myself, give myself pep talks: *This is not going to go away.*"

Then the Chicago Coalition for the Homeless asked her to join its speakers' bureau. Soon she was speaking on panels and meeting with public officials, discovering the power of personal testimony not only to change hearts and minds but ultimately to shape policy and practice. "Putting my story, my pain, into something productive is a way to turn my voice into power," Crystal said. When she saw the impact her story had on others, "The sky just opened up."

Like Crystal, most of the Shrivers said their activism was initially motivated by their own experiences of injustice and inequality, but they all saw that personal experience as a point of entry to a larger struggle. The conversation took flight as they began to imagine what they might achieve together. Jean, a facilitator from California's Silicon Valley De-Bug, proposed an exchange program that would allow young activists to learn from one another while experiencing daily life in different parts of the country. Crystal envisioned a national network to end youth homelessness. Alejandro suggested starting with a skill-based convening for youth activists from various backgrounds, where they could talk shop and at the same time "mingle outside our own fields and realize that everything is connected."

We need look no further than these young visionaries to see how personal interactions evolve into networks that, in turn, generate political power for communities. Pedro Lopez, a 2012 Shriver awardee, is one of many examples. Lopez was propelled into the political arena when the Arizona Legislature passed anti-immigrant legislation in 2010. With friends and family members at risk of deportation, he rallied with other students against the bill at the state capitol. Then he put off starting college to become a field organizer with the immigration advocacy group and MCF grantee Promise Arizona, honing his leadership skills through Promise Arizona's New American Leaders Project, which has trained hundreds of first- and second-generation immigrant leaders to run for elected office. In 2012, Lopez ran for a seat on the Cartwright school board in West Phoenix. At age twenty, he became the youngest person ever to serve on a school board in the state of Arizona.

Lopez is one of a rapidly expanding cadre of grassroots leaders who are coming into power with the support of MCF grantees. At last count, fully one-third of our grantees were actively preparing community members for elected or appointed positions. In a trajectory we see quite often, someone comes in a grantee's door as a client, picks up the advocacy bug, and becomes a community leader—not one who is in it for personal gain but one who is determined to use the power of their role for the good of the community.

When MCF made our initial commitment to cross-issue movement building, the Shriver award winners were in grade school. Today, their deep curiosity about one another's lives, their zeal to connect across issues both personally and politically, and their intuitive understanding of the politics of movement building offer a living example of the ideals we have fought for since our inception.

At the 2016 Shriver gathering, Cesar, an advocate with Asian Americans Advancing Justice, said something I will always remember: "Let's establish a connection and *then* start on the work." These strike me as words to live by in divisive times. They characterize a new generation of changemakers not yet entrenched in the single-issue ethos of the movements of past decades. These great movements—the civil rights movement, the women's movement, the farmworkers' movement, the LGBTQ rights movement, and more—created space for the aspirations of this new generation but do not circumscribe them. In the cross-issue efforts of these dedicated young activists I find a consoling counterpoint to the zero-sum, us vs. them spirit that drives so much of the current political climate. More than that, in their shared energy and deep commitment to collective action, I see a source of tremendous power.

"I am a youth leader"

"*Hola, buenas tardes*. My name is Edna Lizbeth Chavez, and I am from South Los Angeles, California, *el sur de Los Ángeles*."

I did not know the speaker personally, but the voice on the radio had a familiar cadence and intensity that caught my ear instantly. I turned on the television to see a seventeen-year-old girl with long, dark hair commanding the podium as if it were her birthright at the youth-led anti-gun March for Our Lives in Washington, D.C. A few sentences in and her directness and intensity had the crowd of hundreds of thousands—gathered to protest gun violence in the wake of the Parkland, Florida, shootings—shouting and cheering. Thinking back to myself at her age, when speaking to a classroom of strangers made my knees shake, I marveled at her confidence and wondered where it came from.

Very quickly, I got my answer, as Chavez went on to introduce herself as a youth leader at South Central Youth Empowered thru Action, a project of the Los Angeles–based Community Coalition. Community Coalition was one of MCF's first grantees. In fact, my very first site visit brought me to their Los Angeles office. It was the height of the crack epidemic and the neighborhood was bleak, with liquor stores on every corner, but the Community

Coalition offices were filled with life and energy—seniors, teen-agers, grandparents caring for grandchildren, and more filled the building. I met with a young physician assistant named Karen Bass, who had founded the organization out of concern that a combination of drugs and over-policing was destroying her community. The organization she was building, she told me, was born explicitly as a black/brown alliance with the goal of "organizing the community to turn despair and hopelessness into action." She was particularly concerned about the youth in the neighborhood, who she felt were unfairly demonized while their many strengths went ignored and untapped.

Today, Karen Bass is a member of the U.S. House of Repre-sentatives and head of the Congressional Black Caucus, and Community Coalition is a thriving, multipronged organization committed to building civic power, with a focus on youth leader-ship. That is why Chavez's voice sounded so familiar to me—not because I had heard this young woman before, but because I was intimately familiar with all the work, generations' worth, that stood behind her—all the arms that had joined to help lift her to this stage on this day and infused her with the conviction and confidence to rivet a crowd.

"I *am* a youth leader," Chavez shouted, to deafening applause. "I am a survivor. I have lived in South L.A. my entire life and have lost many loved ones to gun violence. This is normal, nor-mal to the point that I have learned to duck from bullets before I learned how to read."

She spoke wrenchingly of losing her brother to the gun vio-lence that plagued her neighborhood—of watching his skin go from brown to grey after he was shot and killed. "Ricardo was his name," she told the crowd. "Can y'all say it with me?" Ricardo's name filled the air, ringing on a thousand lips. At that moment, I saw that Chavez had the organizer's gift: turning many voices into one.

"I am not alone in this experience," she continued. "For decades, my community of South Los Angeles has become accustomed to this violence. It is normal to see candles. It is normal to see posters. It is normal to see balloons. It is normal to see flowers honoring the lives of black and brown youth that have lost their lives to a bullet."

Then she deftly pivoted from the personal to the political: no more police in the schools, she insisted; no more criminalizing black and brown students rather than making them safer. Instead, she called for restorative justice, mentorship, mental health resources, job opportunities, and other initiatives to tackle root causes of violence in her neighborhood and many others. "So, let's make it happen," she concluded briskly. "It's important to work with people that are impacted by these issues—the people you represent."

Listening to Chavez mesmerize a crowd in the hundreds of thousands underscored for me the importance of looking to the natural leadership that exists within communities. The term "leader" should not be reserved for elected officials, non- or for-profit CEOs, or, for that matter, foundation executives. The mother who joins the PTA at her child's school to address educational inequities and advocate for struggling students is a leader. The bilingual teen who accompanies his parents to canvass neighborhoods, serving as an interpreter and discussing voting, pollution, or asthma rates is a leader. The parent who has two minimum-wage jobs but takes time to volunteer at a nonpartisan phone bank to remind neighbors to vote is a leader. Together, they represent the kind of power MCF is dedicated to building.

MCF grantees do not merely address families as clients or beneficiaries; they engage families as partners and constituents. Almost two-thirds of our grantees have families participating as employees or board members. In partnership with their constituents, grantees are leading policy change at all levels of decision making—school boards, city councils, state and national legislatures, and the private sector.

MCF's commitment to listening to our grantees and their constituents before we act does not magically eradicate the power imbalance that comes along with an endowment. But it does go a long way toward neutralizing the power struggles that can make relationships between funders and grantees so fraught. By supplanting "power over" with "power together," we nourish the work and allow it to flourish. Power in this context is measured not by the "wins" we accomplish in the moment but by the empowered communities that make those victories possible—communities that are writing their own agenda for lasting change.

Chapter 11: The Road Ahead

If there is no struggle, there is no progress.

—*Frederick Douglass*

Two decades into an intensive effort to nurture a family-led movement to fight poverty, I find myself returning again and again to the same questions: What lies ahead? What will it take to eradicate racial and economic injustice once and for all and force this country to live up to its ideals and its potential?

The larger economic context is not encouraging. The years since the Marguerite Casey Foundation was founded have seen a stunning accumulation of wealth in the hands of a very few, while the median income has remained stagnant, and the number of families living below the federal poverty line has risen, from 24 million in 2002 to more than 25 million in 2018. Most troubling is the increase in families living in what I can only call dire poverty. In 2017, according to the Children's Defense Fund (CDF), nearly 5.9 million children—about one in twelve—lived in extreme poverty, defined as an annual income of less than half the poverty level. That's less than $12,642 a year for a family of four, or $35 a day to cover the expenses of an entire family. As with poverty in general, these numbers reflect troubling racial disparities: the CDF reports that nearly one in six American Indian/Alaska Native children, more than one in seven black children, and one in ten Hispanic children lives in extreme poverty, compared with one in twenty white children.

It would be easy enough to look at these figures and conclude that we had failed—or, perhaps more reasonably, that the challenge we set for ourselves was an impossible one. But we were never looking for quick fixes. Early on, we made a commitment to nurturing a family-led movement. This means we assess our work on movement time, which history tells us is measured not in years but generations. It means we view our achievements through a movement lens: have we helped mobilize a base that is prepared to fight together for change as they define it? As I look through this lens, I am anything but disheartened.

With an initial endowment of 600 million dollars—little more than the rounding error on a single day's worth of the federal budget—we knew from the start that we did not have the resources to service people out of poverty. But we also understood that poverty is more than a lack of material resources. Poverty is also a lack of power, of social and political capital, and of a public voice. On these fronts—all of which are central to movement building—we have made tremendous progress. In the twenty years since MCF was founded, our grantees have engaged millions of adult and youth community members. They have conducted policy campaigns to bring about change from the neighborhood and community to the state, regional, and national levels, achieving concrete wins while building their capacity to improve the well-being of all of America's families. Increasingly, they have done so by working with one another—collaborations the foundation supports through our convenings and Equal Voice Networks. This family engagement, along with the policy and programmatic wins that ensue, is the metric by which we measure our progress.

In 2016 alone, MCF grantees connected with more than 21 million people through house meetings, educational forums, chapter meetings, and town halls. Two million community members spoke out at meetings and public actions. Each year, thousands of committed leaders emerge from these engagements, working at all levels, from organizing a neighborhood watch to serving in Congress. Countless relationships are forged among people from every background imaginable. These connections form the infrastructure on which movements are built.

Consistency may not be flashy, but I believe it is at the heart of our success. As I look back over the work of the past twenty years, I can say with confidence that we have stayed true to our founding commitment to support a cross-issue movement while navigating a political landscape divided by single-issue politics. And we've been at it long enough to see it bear fruit. The fight to raise the minimum wage, for example, which we have supported in multiple states, has lifted the income of more than 5 million Americans, according to the Economic Policy Institute, adding more than 5 billion dollars in additional earnings to the bottom tier of the economy. Many of the same states have also expanded their Earned Income Tax Credit, and some have passed laws mandating paid family leave and expanding access to loan-free higher education. Others have limited the interest rates exploitative payday lenders can charge. Working together, grantees have passed laws and policies stemming the school-to-prison pipeline, restoring the right to vote to those returning home from prison, halting unfair evictions, advancing housing equity, and improving child care. These grassroots victories are too numerous to list, but they all underscore my faith in our grantmaking model and, most of all, our remarkable grantees.

Today, I don't get as many crazy looks when I talk about how families are the unit of change and the source of leadership our country needs. And no one can tell me that families who experience poverty don't have the wisdom and the agency to solve their own problems. Should someone try, I'll happily tick off an extensive list of evidence proving otherwise.

Changing the conversation

I am also proud of the impact we have had on the field of philanthropy. It may have taken two decades, but simply by adhering to our founding values, we have gone from outlier to pioneer. Approaches that were seen as iconoclastic in our early years—a commitment to general support; building and sustaining networks as a key driver of change; movement building; and even something as straightforward as listening to the communities we fund—are increasingly being championed by the larger philanthropic community, including foundations with far greater resources than ours.

When I read philanthropic publications and speak with my colleagues in the field, I see aspects of the MCF approach that initially led many to look at us askance now being widely discussed. When MCF began including community members in all of our convenings, for instance, some of my colleagues were perplexed. Today, it has become common to hear funders talking about the importance of hearing from those most affected when key decisions are made (although putting this value into practice remains inconsistent).

There is also growing interest in long-term general support, the mainstay of our grantmaking practice. Still, we have a long way to go for that interest to translate into consistent practice. Our grantees regularly tell me what a tremendous relief it is to find a funder who understands that they, as local leaders with deep roots in their community, must set their own course if real change is to happen. Yet for many years, MCF's commitment to general support was seen as unsophisticated by many of our fellow grantmakers. Following the siren song of "strategic philanthropy," they focused instead on ever-more specific issue areas and time-limited initiatives—anything but asking those in the community what they needed and then trusting them with the resources to do their work.

Now, as strategic philanthropy loses its cachet, more funders are "discovering" general support. Five of the nation's largest foundations recently made news by announcing that, after two years of study, they had determined that they and their colleagues were not doing enough to cover grantees' operating costs and announced plans to educate the field about the importance of general support.

The shift in the conversation is heartening, but so far, it has not been matched by a parallel shift in grantmaking practices. Virtually all of the elements of the MCF approach have been identified as best practices with a proven track record of success, yet they have not become the norm within philanthropy at large, or even among those foundations that define themselves as social change actors. Even the five foundations that made a public commitment to general support acknowledged that their own grants currently cover just half of a typical grantee's overhead costs. Sector-wide, even as talk of general support is growing, dollars spent on it are not. General support comprised roughly 20 percent of grantmaking dollars spent in 2017, and many funders still provide nothing at all in the way of general support, leaving nonprofits struggling to cover daily expenses. In addition to sending a corrosive message about funders' lack of faith in their grantees' ability to make decisions about how to allocate resources, this "starvation cycle" leaves grantees and their constituents in a precarious financial situation. A 2017 analysis by Bridgespan of 274 nonprofits that received funding from major foundations found that 42 percent had less than three months' worth of cash on hand.

There has also been a significant shift in opinion when it comes to movement building. When MCF first went public with our commitment to supporting social movements, our colleagues expressed shock. Some warned that we were placing ourselves at the "fringes" of the field. Today, the language of movement building is so widespread as to seem unremarkable. Even advertisers have jumped on the bandwagon, with trade publications exhorting companies to "build movements, not campaigns!" and pushing "brand-fueled movements" that capitalize on the language and energy of movement building in order to sell more widgets. The philanthropic press is abuzz as well with enthusiasm for battling inequality by supporting movement building. But again, despite the talk, actual dollars to support movement building remain limited.

I understand all too well the difficulties that come with implementing MCF's core practices. As the *Foundation Review* has pointed out, "Movement building presents unique challenges to foundations. Because movements, by definition, must be driven by the people who are most affected, foundations cannot determine the goals and timetables of a movement." As MCF stayed the course in our efforts to meet these challenges, we have faced consternation not only from other funders but even, in the early years, from some of our grantees, who questioned the role of a funder in the ground-up work of movement building. Would we try to take over, or position ourselves as leaders simply because we controlled a funding stream? As we made it clear again and again, through actions as well as words, that we had no interest in setting the agenda ourselves, we have gained the trust of those on the ground. But as other funders begin to express interest in movement building, we understand the uphill road they face.

Nevertheless, I remain convinced that if funders practice humility and don't try to lead, we can make a huge difference by lending our resources to the grassroots organizers and activists across the country who *do* have the capacity to determine the goals and strategy of a family-driven movement. My hope is that MCF's success on this front will eventually inspire others to dedicate significant resources to supporting movement building in this country.

Another area where I see progress within philanthropy is in the rising awareness of the importance of working, and funding, across issue. The term "intersectionality" may be relatively new, but out among our grantees, I see it in action day after day—particularly in the growth of the regional Equal Voice Networks. From time to time, I still think of the woman at that early convening who objected to being seated with those outside her field. The attitude her discomfort reflected is far from obsolete, but I do believe the conversation has evolved over the years. Activists on the leading edge of change today are adopting a multi-issue focus and actively seeking ways to work together, and funders are beginning to recognize the power of this approach.

Finally, I have to consider where things stand when it comes to an issue that is deeply personal to me: what is referred to in the field as "Diversity, Equity, and Inclusion" or simply DEI. I am immensely proud of the community we have built at MCF, where 80 percent of the board and 60 percent of the staff are people of color, and 78 percent of grantees are organizations of color (which we define on the basis of the diversity of board, staff, and leadership). By consistently hiring and promoting women and people of color and building one of the most diverse boards in philanthropy, I believe MCF has contributed to an essential shift in the field. When I was hired as president and CEO of the Marguerite Casey Foundation, I was the first Latina to head a major national foundation and one of a handful of women of color in the CEO role. Today, according to the Chicago Foundation for Women, there are twenty women of color heading foundations in that city alone. These leaders are not only evidence of transformation—they are the agents of transformation and will be well into the future.

While I am heartened by the existence of this new generation of leaders, the work is far from complete. Given that only 15 percent of foundation trustees, and fewer than 10 percent of foundation CEOs, are people of color, is it any surprise that just 10 percent of domestic funding goes to people of color—a number that has barely budged since MCF was founded? We have many miles to go as a field before we can even begin to claim to be reflecting the diversity that is America, much less serving those communities most in need.

The future of philanthropy

Even as I look back at the road we have traveled so far, I also find myself looking ahead, contemplating the future not only of MCF but of philanthropy as a whole. I believe we are at a crucial juncture as we grapple with the impact of rising inequality. The extent of poverty in America is not only a humanitarian crisis, it is a moral outrage. At the same time, great fortunes are being built—fortunes that are the wellspring of philanthropy itself. How do we reconcile these dual realities?

One thing is clear: it is not enough for an ever-smaller, ever-richer clan of oligarchs to extract all the wealth and then give some back as charity and call it a day. The longer I spend in the field of philanthropy, the more concerned I become about its remarkable ability to concentrate both capital and power. Until we start asking hard questions about equity and the distribution of resources in this country, we haven't begun to do our job.

The good news is that we *are*, as a field, beginning to ask questions about the relationship between philanthropy and outrageous wealth. This is a crucial conversation that I am heartened to see taking place among many of my colleagues. At the same time, as a field we have yet to come up with concrete strategies that will enable us to balance our commitment to the donors who make our work possible with our larger commitment to advancing the common good.

Doing so is not going to be easy because it requires challenging longstanding beliefs and practices. Philanthropic dollars, the traditional thinking goes, flow from the hands of well-intentioned elites into the endowments of wisely run institutions, which proudly bear the family name while promoting the public good. With wealth, this analysis presumes, comes wisdom, so philanthropic benefactors are ideally situated to decide how huge sums are spent.

There are a couple of problems with this analysis—long-taboo concerns that are finally beginning to get a hearing. In an age of skyrocketing inequality, vast fortunes have created philanthropies of almost unfathomable resources and power. In this context, critics are beginning to ask questions about whether the wealthy, however beneficent their intentions, should have such unchecked power over local and national priorities. Why should those who have benefited most from the inequities of capitalism have the loudest voice in the conversation about how resources should be distributed in the name of social good?

The fact that wealth and wisdom do not always align may be the more obvious concern, but to my mind, it is not the most significant problem. My great concern—which is only growing alongside the massive fortunes of the Internet era—is that the tax deduction that comes with large-scale philanthropy allows donors to "give away" their money while retaining near-total control over how it is spent. The problem with this way of doing things is that the roughly 40 percent of their income that the very rich would otherwise be compelled, by progressive taxation, to use for the public good is virtually exempt from public oversight. Donors may part ways with their cash, but for all intents and purposes, they retain the power associated with it. Unlike other institutions that operate in the name of the common good, foundations are essentially accountable to no one.

It has long struck me that the portion of a foundation's endowment that comes from untaxed profits rightfully belongs to the public and should be allocated with the public good in mind.

Too often, however, philanthropic dollars are used to burnish the name and reputation of the giver, or even to garner personal advantage for those who already have more than their share.

No one, philanthropists included, eagerly submits to greater oversight, and we in this field have long been accustomed to operating with very few constraints. But we need to start thinking more deeply about the obligations that come along with our significant tax break. This starts with challenging the sacrosanct nature of donor intent. If the common good is defined exclusively by the donor, where is the commonality? Should the goals and desires of wealthy white men from a century or two ago—or, for that matter, those who garnered their fortunes more recently—truly be guiding billions of dollars in untaxed spending? What voice should the most neglected communities—those whose labor in large part fuels these fortunes but who see so little of the proceeds—have in the distribution of those untaxed profits? And what about the taxpayers? If I contribute even a penny of my own tax dollars to offset those you did not pay because you started a foundation, shouldn't I have some voice in how that money is spent? I may not approve of the way my government spends my tax dollars, but at least I have some power to influence it with my vote. Foundations are subject to no such constraints.

I am aware that it is not up to me to decide how other funders spend their money. But the 40 percent of charitable funds that would otherwise go to taxes are not truly "their money." Those particular dollars are *our* money, as a society, and decisions about how best to allocate them should be made accordingly. I would like to see a mechanism in place to ensure that dispersals from the portion of philanthropic endowments that would otherwise go to taxes be made not by private boards but by entities that are accountable to the public and include representatives of multiple communities. More concretely, I am proposing that foundations place whatever portion of their assets would otherwise be paid in taxes in a separate box—call it an "equity trust"—which would be governed not by a traditional board of directors but by a community board whose members would be drawn from those communities most in need of philanthropic support. Short of legislation mandating such a shift, I would challenge my fellow philanthropists to make it voluntarily.

As I look to the future, there is another concrete development I hope to see in place: a membership organization that unites the voices of low-income families to advance their shared interests in the political arena. I strongly believe that such an organization is needed to formalize the aspirations of families and garner the political power to move the dial at the highest levels of government. In 2015, MCF ventured into this space by incorporating Equal Voice Action (EVA), a national 501(c)(4) membership organization focused on building the political power of poor and low-income families. A 501(c)(4) can engage in more advocacy, lobbying, and other political activities than can a traditional nonprofit. This is important because we know that politicians respond to identifiable, organized voting blocs, and poor families have yet to be recognized as such. As Ruth Massinga, who first proposed a membership organization, put it, "When poor families have what AARP is to retired people and the NRA is to gun owners, that will be the culmination of our work."

Over this time, I have become acutely aware of how difficult it is to bring this immense vision to fruition. Ultimately, we came to the conclusion that building a national membership organiza-

tion was perhaps an idea ahead of its time and thus we decided
to sunset EVA. But Ruth's words still ring true to me today. Our
experiment left me more convinced than ever that our most
ambitious goals will only be achieved when we are able to see
past the barriers that divide us. At the end of the day, I will not
be satisfied until poor people have political power and are heard,
and that will only happen when they are united in a formal way.
I remain convinced that a membership organization is critical to
making that happen, wherever it is housed and whatever structure it ultimately takes.

When I assess our progress so far, more than anything else,
I see faces—those of the thousands of family members across
the country who have discovered their own power and raised
their shared voices to demand the changes that *they*, not we,
have determined they need. When I contemplate the changes
this work has wrought in how they see themselves and their own
collective power, I feel enormous pride. Most of all, I feel great
hope for the future, even at a moment when hope feels hard to
come by.

The power of family

Even as our grantees are changing the world, their relationships
with one another—fostered with intention through our networks and convenings—are changing the way they see and do
their own work. I can think of many examples, but Josh Hoyt,
executive director of the National Partnership for New Americans, has stayed in my mind because of his vivid account of how
attending one of our national Equal Voice convenings in 2007

transformed his perspective on his own work within the immigration rights movement, and ultimately influenced the field as a whole.

In the years before the convening, Hoyt told me, the immigration wars were heating up, fueled by ugly rhetoric conflating immigrants with criminals and legislation that institutionalized that perspective. "We saw nightly attacks on CNN over 'illegal criminals,' the rise of the Minutemen carrying arms to protect the border from the 'invasion by illegals,'" Hoyt recalled. The immigrant rights movement responded to this hateful rhetoric by framing its message as "Immigrants are workers, not criminals." The message was crafted to push back against the demonization of immigrants, Hoyt said, but "little thought was put into the fact that we were accepting the frame of criminalization, or what that meant to other groups who were victims of the massive prison industrial complex, especially African Americans."

Then Hoyt came to the national Equal Voice convening in Chicago, where he spent time with a multiracial, intergenerational group of activists from across the country. The table where Hoyt sat included two formerly incarcerated black women, two young Korean sisters who were immigrant college students and a middle-aged Latino couple with strong religious values. The black women spoke of trying to keep custody of their children after being released from prison. The Korean women talked about being undocumented and how one of them and their brother had been held by ICE in a detention center. Finally, the Latino couple shared how their son had made mistakes and was currently in prison for fraud.

"The Equal Voice table conversation was one of the most deeply moving in my forty-two-year organizing career," Hoyt told me. "I was dumbstruck at the power of the 'family' approach to the conversation. It demolished the differences between the participants. It showed how the mass incarceration and criminalization approach to both criminal justice and to immigration had touched everyone in the group. It united us across race. I left there, and my organization changed our organizing framework from 'Workers, not Criminals' to 'Protect Families.' I have carried your core message about families through all of my work ever since."

Hoyt shared the evolution in his thinking with his allies in the immigration rights movement, many of whom also went on to adopt a family frame. Not for the first time, nor for the last, family voices had ripple effects locally, regionally, and nationally. This is the kind of trajectory I've seen again and again, as family members and nonprofit leaders from every background get the chance to meet one another and work together to advance shared concerns. Building a multi-issue movement in a silo-driven world has been and will continue to be a challenge. But stories like Hoyt's—and there are many—leave me tremendously proud of the progress we have made simply by staying true to our original commitment. Over the years I have seen MCF grantees work together to move the dial on so many crucial fronts: living wage laws, immigration rights, affordable housing, child care, criminal justice, voting rights, and much more. These victories are tangible proof that empowered, connected communities can change circumstances that might otherwise seem immutable.

When I look back at the past twenty years, I am humbled and amazed by the progress our grantees have made together: the thousands of family voices they have brought together; the armies of formidable grassroots leaders they have cultivated; the bridges they have built amongst one another; and the mountains they have moved on the policy front, improving the daily lives of countless families. Every day, I see our grantees working across lines of difference, learning from each other's struggles and building on each other's victories in a shared effort to roll back poverty and advance equity. Together, they are a powerful force to be reckoned with.

At the same time, as we approach the most bitterly partisan election I can remember, it is all too easy to imagine a starkly divided future for this country—indeed, for the globe. But to accept that divided future would be to give in to the exhaustion of despair. Fortunately, in the voices of the committed activists and organizers I speak with every day, exhaustion is not what I hear. Division is not what I see. Instead, I sense a growing commitment to working together across boundaries of race, region, ego, and—perhaps most importantly—issue to ensure an equitable future for all of us.

One of my own strongest memories of my early years as an immigrant in the United States was the day Richard Nixon resigned from the presidency. I was at James Lick Junior High School when the news broke. Within half an hour, the school secretary came to my classroom and called me to the office. My father was there along with my younger sisters, all looking scared and confused. My father told me to gather my belongings; we were going home.

Later, I came to understand that he was concerned there would be fighting in the streets, and our family would not be safe unless we were together. Coming from Central America, he had never experienced an unexpected shift in power without some kind of violence or even civil war. He had grown up with the understanding that if a leader was toppled, you gathered your family and whatever possessions you could carry and headed for the mountains. He simply could not imagine a peaceful transfer of power.

I think of that day often because it reminds me of what I love about this country and how deeply I believe in the promise of democracy. I may be an immigrant, but I still have the right to tell you what I think. You may not like that—you may not like *me*—but I'm not going to be put in jail for expressing my opinion. This is the America I am willing to fight for, even as I challenge those aspects of our culture that strike me as inequitable, unjust, or simply wrong.

I have to keep fighting for this nation to live up to its values, because I have a stake in our collective future. I have skin in the game—my own skin through my grandchildren. I have to believe that they are going to be part of something better—that they will raise their own children in the beautiful democracy that draws people to America from all over the globe. There is a movement building out there, the kind that leaves in its wake a transformed world. I may not live to see it, but my grandchildren will. It's going to be a hell of a fight getting there, but this is what I believe.

When I contemplate the future to which I aspire, I think of the Exodus scene in the 1956 Charlton Heston film *The Ten Commandments*, when the Israelites finally leave slavery together. I first watched it as a child, and although I may not have understood exactly what I was seeing, I could feel the powerful momentum beneath the clamor of pots and pans, broken carts, old people, and children herding flocks of geese. What makes this scene so evocative for me is that everyone gathers under the banner of their particular tribe, but they all march together toward a freedom they are just beginning to imagine. That is my vision of a movement—people of all backgrounds, preserving and honoring those backgrounds but at the same time walking together, working together, toward a shared future.

I have always seen movement building as a journey rather than a destination. We know where we are headed—toward a world where everyone has what they need to raise their children without fear of hunger or cold—but as poet Antonio Machado so evocatively writes, "the road is made by walking." We don't know when we will reach our destination, or even that we will, but the road we are building together as we march side by side is beautiful in itself, smoothed by thousands of footsteps and ringing with thousands of voices joined together in laughter, argument, and song. We know, as we walk it, that none of us walks alone.

Acknowledgments

I have been blessed to work with so many passionate, talented, and dedicated thought leaders throughout my career in philanthropy. I will be forever grateful for their guidance, support, and encouragement as we built this new philanthropy from the ground up.

Ruth Massinga, president and CEO of Casey Family Programs, for her fearlessness, strength, and clarity in creating a unique foundation that spoke truth to power.

My "fab four" founding board members: Dr. Freeman Hrabowski, Dr. Douglas Patiño, Patricia Schroeder, and Dr. William (Bill) Foege for their collaboration, wisdom, and heartfelt commitment to bettering the lives of low-income families and specifically people of color.

Freeman, you are a trusted colleague, mentor, and loving brother. If every president and board chair shared the alchemy we have, I have no doubt that the field of philanthropy would be transformed tomorrow.

Douglas, you have been responsible for so much of what this foundation has been able to accomplish. You are a dear friend and trusted partner.

Pat, my smart and courageous colleague—you have been a trailblazer in advancing women's rights, and your support over the years has meant the world to me.

Bill, you were forever our humble, kind, brilliant, and funny professor in residence at every board meeting. I always waited for your customary three points and the insightful commentary that followed.

Thanks to my other stellar Marguerite Casey Foundation board members: Melody Barnes, Chad Boettcher, Dr. Angela Diaz, Tessie Guillermo, Dr. Rami Nashashibi, Dr. Carmen Rojas, Dr. Jack Thomas, and David Villa.

My deepest thanks to all of the grantee families, partners, and organizations we at MCF have had the pleasure of working with over the years. It has been our privilege to walk with you on the road of justice and social change. Even as we celebrate local, regional, and national policy wins together, we must remain vigilant, as so much more needs to be done.

MCF staff, current and past, whose hard work, talent, and commitment to empowering families fuels the foundation's daily work.

I have been part of a philanthropic CEO cohort for the last six years. It has been a space to discuss issues and concerns and become leaders better equipped for the challenges of creating and managing a diverse workforce. Gratitude to my cohort colleagues: Susan Anderson, Doug Stamm, Diane Kaplan, Kris Hermanns, Liz Vivian, Max Williams, and Richard Woo.

Dr. Bob Ross and Stephen Heintz, my D5 co-chairs and partners in building diversity, equity, and inclusion in the field of philanthropy. I thank you for using your prominent perches to lead by example and bring more people of color into the field.

Several trusted colleagues gave me astute, critical, and gentle feedback on the manuscript: Dr. Freeman Hrabowski, Dr. Rami Nashashibi, Chad Boettcher, James Head, Peggy Saika, Diana Campoamor, Crystal Hayling, and Susana (Nini) Vega.

Irene Schleicher offered invaluable assistance at every step of the way, shepherding this book through to its completion with a keen eye.

Sincere thanks to Julie Enszer, my editor at Jacques Books, an imprint of The New Press, for believing in this book. The New Press is a book publisher with a social justice mission and, as they say, "a big vision: to change the world, book by book." I am honored to be an author under their imprint.

Special thanks to Nell Bernstein, who has been involved in countless publications that MCF has produced since 2002. Without her collaboration, this book would not have been possible.

To my brilliant successor, Dr. Carmen Rojas, who I know will continue to build on the foundation's legacy and take it to the next level.

Finally, to Mrs. Gloria Burchard, my high school teacher, who saw my potential and not only encouraged me to apply to college but paid my college application fee. I hope that every child has at least one teacher in their life who makes this kind of difference.

Index